PRAISE FOR *DEAR ERMA BOMBECK IN HEAVEN – WHAT THE HELL?!*

"This book is so funny, sharp, and sweet, I'm angry I didn't write it myself."

Mike Reiss, Emmy-winning writer, producer, and showrunner of *The Simpsons*

"Often times I wonder what my mom would have written about if she were still alive today. Jillian Van Hefty's book, *Dear Erma Bombeck in Heaven – What the Hell?!*, answered that question. Observant and wickedly funny, she takes on aging, plastic surgery, trendy diets, and trendy parents. Anyone can hold a mirror up and show us who we are, but not many have the gift to make us laugh at it."

Matthew Bombeck, son of Erma Bombeck

"I really enjoyed your manuscript, and am convinced my mom would be, or is, laughing as well. *Dear Erma Bombeck in Heaven – What the Hell?!* will help keep her legacy alive and, most important, people laughing at themselves and life in general."

Andy Bombeck, son of Erma Bombeck

DEAR ERMA BOMBECK IN HEAVEN – WHAT THE HELL?!

JILLIAN VAN HEFTY

Flint Hills Publishing

Dear Erma Bombeck in Heaven –
What the Hell?!

Cover Design by Amy Albright
stonypointgraphics.weebly.com

Flint Hills Publishing
Topeka, Kansas
Tucson, Arizona
www.flinthillspublishing.com

Paperback ISBN: 978-1-966323-55-6
Hardcover ISBN: 978-1-966323-57-0
Electronic Book ISBN: 978-1-966323-56-3

Library of Congress Control Number 2026902008

Printed in the U.S.A.

I dedicate this book to all the mothers who never get proper credit for anything.

And to anyone who ever clipped Erma's newspaper column to their refrigerator—and who hasn't?—

I miss her too.

CONTENTS

ARE YOU THERE, ERMA? IT'S ME

Dear Erma,

Don't worry, this isn't an invitation to a destination wedding, a team building exercise at an escape room, or worst of all, a wine sip-and-paint class.

I'm just an average wife and stay-at-home mom (a misnomer because I actually live at Sam's Club) so confounded by the zany trends, contemporary nuisances, and pop-culture changes taking place since you passed thirty years ago, my swear jar receives an annual W-4.

You once wrote, "If you can't make it better, you can laugh at it." My hope is that by writing letters to you as you laugh at us in heaven, the farrago of WTFs, eye rolls, and barf emojis that have become commonplace in my life will be replaced by the humor you were (and still are!) known for.

Yours truly,

Me

P.S. By the way, I am one of the few remaining people who still writes letters on actual paper and sends them through the mail.

P.P.S. Wait, you *did* make it to heaven, right?

WELCOME TO THIS BANANAS WORLD, BABY RUTABAGA

Dear Erma,

I commend you and your husband, Bill, for giving your children sensible names. Betsy, Andrew, and Matthew are classics! Parents today are more likely to call their newborns North, South, East, or West than Matthew, Mark, Luke, or John. And when they do pick classic names, David becomes Davydd, Jason becomes Jacesynn, Michael becomes Mykkel, and Victoria becomes Vykktoryheough.

Trendy moms and dads gather inspiration from the unlikeliest of sources and name their offspring after herbs and spices, chic cities, luxury cars, and the eye chart at the optometrist's office. My young son, George, rides the bus with a set of twins, Dez and Cruz, named after deciduous trees and cruciferous vegetables. I've seen a moniker that, in lieu of actual vowels and consonants, had been serialized using an advanced IT password policy requiring special characters and digits. Another was named Vowel, spelled Aeiouandsometimesy. Roll call sounds like Charlie Brown's teacher imitating an Emergency Broadcast System monthly testing drill. The poor teachers need Rosetta Stone and a sign-language interpreter to translate. They spent less time cracking the Enigma Code.

Some believe it's clever to include conception details, but an adolescent named K-Y, JetBlue, or Jacuzzi is bound to be saddled with a bad reputation, legitimate or not. And that's not to mention what will happen to poor Broken Condom and Oopsie.

Others burden their babies with impossible expectations. I knew a couple—both college professors—who expected their daughter, Mediterranean, to excel in linguistics, geography, and spelling simply by learning to write her signature. Unfortunately, the best report card the pitiful thing ever received was her Apgar score.

Then there are the sentimentalists who pay homage to a favorite person or idealistic concept. A birth announcement in the local newspaper read, "Our beloved son was born on Christmas Day. We hope he will be a symbol of peace, love, and joy for the world." You'd have assumed they named him Jesus, but it was "Santuh Clauzz." Santuh Clauzz, incidentally, weighed 12 pounds, 2.5 ounces.

My husband, Hank, went with me to pick up some paint samples. I realized they had the same names as George's classmates: Bone Tinsel, Infinity Shadow, and Dune Summit. Casanova, by all accounts, appeared to be a perfectly nice boy, but I dissuaded George from getting too chummy because I felt uncomfortable saying his name in public. Or in private. Especially in private.

This is such a contrast to when I grew up. My fourth-grade class had twelve Lisas, eleven Curts, ten Dawns, nine Tims, eight Pams, seven Steves, six Pattys, five Chads, four Bonnies, three Todds, two Rhondas, and a Partridge-in-a-Pear-Tree. (His parents were hippies.)

Erma, you once wrote, "One thing they never tell you about child raising is that for the rest of your life, at the drop of a hat, you are expected to know your child's name." When parents get overly original, how can they possibly recall those names? My mom and dad often hollered out for pets, television characters, or other random things when trying to get my attention. "Lassie; Mr. Thurston Howell III; Weebles wobble but they don't fall down; Nanu Nanu; Collect $200 as you pass go; Goodnight, John-Boy; For the love of God, who are you again?" They could easily recall that my bologna had a first name, spelled O-S-C-A-R, but rarely could they remember mine on a whim. In time, the National Hurricane Center will shun names like Helene and Ivan, forcing meteorologists to warn the public of the approaching Category 5 Rogue Swan.

I have never shared this with anyone, Erma, but I've always secretly hoped that George will name his first child after me. The way trends are headed, it will be my *essence* that is honored. I can see it now: *Laughing Cow Creamy Original Cheese Wedge* will be number 7,981 on the Social Security Administration's list of most popular baby names of 2050. It's even unisex!

Yours truly,

Me

WHEN "THREE BLIND MICE" BECOMES A THREE-RING-CIRCUS

Dear Erma,

You once wrote, "You show me a boy who brings a snake home to his mother, and I'll show you an orphan." That is exactly how I feel about the drums. Thank goodness, George has the good sense not to even try.

About a month ago, however, he did come home with another instrument. His teacher's note read, "Congratulations on beginning your musical journey! I am excited to introduce the extraordinary, beautiful, and historic recorder. Please encourage twenty minutes of practice daily in preparation for our upcoming performance. We find assigning a name fosters a meaningful relationship with the auditory arts." George called his recorder Barbara.

Barbara cost six dollars, not including the required sheet music of "Frère Jacques" and "Hot Cross Buns." Overall, she was less expensive and demanding of his time than I expected his first gal pal might be, so I fully approved of their frequently offbeat relationship.

My heart burst with nostalgia when he pulled the scarlet

beauty from her flimsy, opaque sleeve. It was the exact candy-apple color as items from his childhood not so long ago: his Radio Flyer wagon; Etch A Sketch; Curious George's shirt; McDonald's Happy Meal boxes; the balloon in *Goodnight Moon.* Remember all those precious things?

I had to remind myself that George was no longer a tyke. He was a young man—a serious musician with incomprehensible (yet undiscovered) talent. Instead, I focused on iconic red accessories belonging to legendary rock-and-rollers: David Bowie's fiery lighting bolt painted on his face; Elton John's whimsical, rosy spectacles; Joan Jett's cardinal leather jacket; Jimmy Page's crimson, double-neck Gibson guitar; Bruce Springsteen's faded cap tucked into the back pocket of his Levi's. *That will be him and Barbara one day,* I just knew it!

Hank and I approached the auditorium and spotted a large sign that read:

> TONIGHT'S "TALENT EXPLOSION" IS SPONSORED BY MIRACLE-EAR. PLEASE BE AWARE THAT SPECIAL EFFECTS USING STROBE LIGHTS AND FLASHING IMAGES WILL BE USED DURING THIS PERFORMANCE. PATRONS THAT SUFFER FROM EPILEPSY, MIGRAINES, OR ARE AT RISK OF PRETERM LABOR ARE ADVISED TO PROCEED WITH CAUTION.

I worried we had mistakenly set foot inside a 1975 roller rink, Space Mountain, or the Las Vegas Strip.

I am not epileptic or pregnant, and the only migraine I have experienced was from watching the Australian breakdancer mimicking a kangaroo during the 2024 summer Olympics, so I felt safe to head in. While parents, grandparents, aunts, and uncles made small talk, younger siblings and cousins had tablets glued to their laps.

The velvet curtains parted, and the performers, dressed in their Sunday best, walked single file across the stage to their seats. When his teacher stepped onto her platform and elegantly suspended her hands in the air, the audience hushed to complete silence. George sat erect, enthusiastic, eager; Barbara met his lips. My heart beat like a metronome on the prestissimo setting. I felt an unexpected kinship toward stage mothers, whom I had always secretly judged.

Suddenly, the shrillness of 124 demonic recorders ricocheted off the metal bleachers and cinderblock walls. A real migraine came on fast and strong, and entirely different red images appeared in my mind: a sucking chest wound, a stick of dynamite, conjunctivitis, my car's check engine light, REDRUM scrawled on a door.

Psalms 98:4-6 states, "Make a joyful noise unto the Lord." Talk about creative license.

In an instant, my fantasy of George's career came to a blistering end. "Three Blind Mice" would have been more aptly titled "Four-Hundred Deaf Relatives." I prayed that the flashing lights would kick in any second and send someone—anyone—into preterm labor to put an end to this showcase of tormented banshees. But I had a feeling they would simply drown out the wails of delivery and the crying baby, who would forever flinch at the slightest squeak. In desperation, I scanned the audience hoping to find the Coldplay kiss cam couple to use as a distraction.

I wonder if the Department of Education puts parents through such agony in a push to homeschool. There must be a curriculum less assaulting to one's eardrums. Why not teach miming, ant-farming, or shadow-puppetry? Vaping is a quiet activity.

I reflected on my first concert. My classmates, many of them farmers, showed up in the same overalls worn to milk the cows, and their Mucks left a trail of manure across the gymnasium floor. The performance lasted ten minutes, tops.

Tickets weren't sold via Apple Pay. Tuxedoed ushers didn't distribute trifold programs printed on linen stationery. Aerial videographers didn't hover drones to capture live footage. Sign-language interpreters didn't translate. Parents sure didn't gift bouquets of roses wrapped in kraft paper. Hell, my dad stayed in the car listening to Paul Harvey's *The Rest of the Story* on the radio and missed the entire show.

Whatever happened to Betsy, Andrew, and Matt's recorders, Erma? I bet on the way home after every concert, you chucked them out the car window, and to this day tiny red shards litter the streets surrounding the school. Maybe that was how mosaic art originated.

Do you think I will miss Barbara one day when George enrolls in band and introduces me to a louder, more obnoxious, curvier gal with steely looks? Perhaps a trumpet, saxophone, or baritone horn? Erma, please don't be a snake and say, "The drums." *NEVER!*

Yours truly,

Me

WHO ARE THE SOCIOPATHS IN YOUR NEIGHBORHOOD?

Dear Erma,

My family lives in a cookie-cutter suburban development with houses having as much differentiation as the late Hugh Hefner's girlfriends—gorgeous but completely lacking originality.

For starters, every structure is painted within the fifty-shades-of-gray color palette. Even the centralized mailbox hub looks like a miniature mausoleum that stores everyone's individuality. The homes are built so close together that I suck in my gut when passing between them. My neighbor can scan my BoxTops for Education barcodes from her foyer. One night after I made a spicy curry for dinner, she popped over with a small package. "Fences make good neighbors," she said, "but so does GasX."

Our realtor pointed out these potential nuisances during the showing, but I was too enamored with the French doors on the she-shed to notice. To be fair, I shouldn't complain because, after all, the neighborhood is safe. George has left his bike, pogo stick, metal detector, hoverboard, and even himself on the front lawn overnight without being stolen. Nothing more than a notice from the HOA.

Did you know that in 2015, your former Centerville, Ohio home was added to the National Register of Historic Places? What an honor! I promise to keep this secret … tell me about the neighbors who drove you bonkers. Of course, I bet many were afraid to cross you for fear of being mentioned in your column. I wield no such power, so allow me to introduce some of these delightful individuals. As you once wrote, "Some say our national pastime is baseball. Not me. It's gossip."

#1000, the Anderson-Cooper's-hair-colored house: The association board president lives in this former model home. Her favorite hobby is writing people up for arbitrary code violations; she recently imposed a $150 fine to me for singing off-key to my *Hamilton* soundtrack and another $100 for dancing to it. (George and Barbara received $300 in punitive damages for disturbing the peace, which I concede was fair.)

#1028, the ET-when-he-was-dying-colored house: This vegan meanders over to our patio whenever we grill burgers to offer his *Forks Over Knives* documentary on Blu-Ray. So committed is he to his dietary lifestyle that the mere mention of meat is offensive. Instead of slapping the salami, this guy jokes about tickling the tofu/clenching the cucumber/pulverizing the papaya/zonking the zucchini/blessing the bok choy/and punishing the pickle, none of which I am interested in seeing through his greige, top-down bottom-up bathroom shades.

#1140, the elementary-school cafeteria-tray-colored house: The foul mouth on this one. If George Carlin is up there blushing, she is the reason. Whenever we cross paths, she yells out, "Hey, bitch," as if a term of endearment. If I had spoken in such a manner, my mom would've treated me to a shot of Dawn dish soap followed by a Palmolive chaser. She also has replaced the word "friend" with "tribe" and "squad" as if her confidantes are Native American cheerleaders.

#1202, the leftover-milk-after-eating-breakfast-cereal-house: I filed a cease-and-desist order to get this blabbermouth to shut up about her air fryer. *How can you live without one? It will change your life, blah blah blah.* Never since the pressure cooker in *Fatal Attraction* has a kitchen gadget been so obsessed over. She's just as relentless discussing pickleball and Mahjong.

#1222, the Simon Cowell's-T-shirt-on-*American-Idol-The-X-Factor-US*-and-*America's-Got-Talent*-colored house: Boy oh boy, this sales rep has some unbelievable deals waiting. Silpada, Avon, Norwex, Thirty-One gifts, Young Living, and Tupperware—you name it. Just last week she told me I was an "ideal candidate" to join her growing team. The only time I've ever been called that was for my dentist's lifetime teeth-whitening program, until they cut me for lack of commitment.

#1298, the Simon-Cowell's-T-shirt-on-*Pop-Idol-The-X-Factor-UK*-and-*Britain's-Got-Talent*-colored house: The nerve of these folks. They started both a GoFundMe *and* a meal train. *For themselves.* Their pet Netherland Dwarf rabbit needs Invisalign to correct an overbite, and they expect everyone to contribute cash and make a pot roast (except for the guy punishing the pickle).

#1355, the dental-X-rays-with-loads-of-amalgam-fillings-colored house: It's a mystery who lives here, other than three feral beasts that bark incessantly and leave poop landmines all over the unkept yard. I speak for the entire neighborhood by wishing their Invisible Fence was actually visible.

#1358, the oxidized-avocado-colored house: Rainbow-Brite provides daily inspirational messages in sidewalk chalk. Today is a pastel wasp with "BEE yourself!" written in gigantic bubble letters. In third grade, my poem titled, "I Belong in the Partridge Family Instead of My Own" won first place, but despite my literary talent, you don't see me desecrating public property with catchy phrases. Now I feel bad—she is genuinely nice because she takes her own advice to bee herself.

#1366, the Marty McFly's-DeLorean-colored house: Praise be! This child of God has found the Lord our savior and invites all lost souls to join her in worship on Sunday mornings at 10 o'clock (and please bring a non-perishable food item to send to Uganda). Her church's offering tray is now equipped with a chip reader. The 3% credit card fee was approved by Jesus (according to Paul's letters to Visa).

#1370, the Leaning-Tower-of-Pisa-colored house: This unabashed throuple was recently featured on *Dr. Phil,* a ploy, I believe, designed to increase their OnlyFans viewership. Above their fireplace is a portrait of them wearing nothing but Love Your Melons beanie caps.

#1388, the Jabba-the-Hutt-colored house: Oh dear, the TMI family. Everyone in the county knows all about her chronic yeast infections, his multiple bankruptcies, and their teenage son's *Call of Duty* addiction and hence, habitual absenteeism. The boy's name: Truant Einstein.

#1400, the shiitake-mushroom-colored house: This cuckoo coordinates the city-wide garage sale each spring. I would rather reside in North Korea than have a Jeep owner with a plastic ducky cult sprawled across its dashboard park atop my perennials, then haggle me over a John Denver 8-track. ("Annie's Song" alone is worth more than fifty cents.)

Sometimes I wonder how others view me. My guess is that behind their gray doors, within their gray walls, and beneath their gray roof, they refer to me as the gray-haired lady with the gray circles under her eyes who always wears the same gray sweats. Sounds about right, no gray area there.

Yours truly,

Me

DO THESE SKINNY JEANS MAKE MY RESCUE HAMSTER LOOK FAT?

Dear Erma,

There's a dead hamster in my freezer. Well, of course he's dead. I do not know why I felt the need to clarify. In case you're wondering, he died of natural causes before being placed there—I am not that cruel.

George's announcement that he wanted a pet was the verbal equivalent of a white van with tinted windows stalking me on a deserted road. I sensed immediate danger and felt desperate to escape as quickly as possible.

When he pressed the matter, I had him check out a library book titled *Snapping Turtles Need Cuddles Too,* penned by a one-armed, glass-eyed herpetologist. (Contrary to what my Great Aunt Maude says, a herpetologist is not a sexually transmitted disease specialist at The Villages retirement community in Florida.) I figured my plan would put an end to the subject because he was excited about attending canoe camp the upcoming summer and wouldn't dare risk losing extremities.

I also learned something interesting. Turtles can live to be a hundred years old. The thing would survive all of us. Hank and I were not willing to amend our wills to include a trust fund for a reptile and prosthetics for Laughing Cow Creamy Original Cheese Wedge.

You once wrote, "Every puppy should have a boy," and we briefly considered getting a dog, but again, the lengthy life expectancy was a deal breaker. Dwarf hamsters, on the other hand, live merely twenty-four months. That was twenty-three months more of a commitment than we cared for, but the things we do for our kids, eh?

The next thing I knew, we were in a pet shop that smelled like the primate section of an underfunded zoo. George didn't notice the stench because his nose was pressed flat against the glass enclosure in search of THE BEST HAMSTER IN THE HISTORY OF THE WORLD! He asked me which I thought was cutest, but with the way they wiggled around, they all looked like creepy Mexican jumping beans. We tried to get a closer look at them, but greasy fingerprints and boogers were smeared everywhere, which prevented us from discerning if they were saying their final goodbyes, procreating, or playing The Floor is Lava.

The warm-blooded creature specialist finally arrived, scooped one into her palm, and plopped it into a Chinese takeout box. The thing scratched at the walls like an insane asylum patient after years in solitary confinement. If Andy DuFresne had such a pet in Shawshank Prison, he would have had that tunnel dug in half the time and been able to enjoy his fortune while still a young man.

Their entire inventory—from freshly hatched polliwogs to

white-bearded dragons on hospice—were labeled "rescues." That manipulative marketing term is tossed around by animal organizations more than hostage negotiation teams and the Coast Guard combined.

We spent the next three hours signing adoption papers more thorough than an immigration sponsor's affidavit of support. *What is my profession? Annual income? Education level? Criminal record? Am I smarter than a fifth grader? Should toilet paper hang over or under? Are clowns funny or scary? Is Diehard a Christmas movie? Does pineapple belong on pizza?* Call me a tightwad, but the thing cost $16.99, which I started to consider a poor return on my investment. And given that Hank and I spend $800 a year on pest control services, the irony was not lost on me.

George sensed my apprehension and promptly referred to the hamster care manual he had placed in the cart along with $156 worth of accessories *(skinny jeans!!!!!!!)*. It read, "Pets are a worthwhile financial responsibility." I felt the word "worthwhile" was subjective but could appreciate his point.

Erma, I have vivid memories of munching on Cracker Jack caramel corn in front of the Hardware Hank, "FREE kittens!" and "FREE puppies!" written in thick magic marker on a tattered Kimbies disposable diaper box. (Poor Bob Barker and his wasted words at the end of the Showcase Showdown: "Reminding you to help control the pet population. Have your pets spayed or neutered." It was as if he was speaking to my town exclusively.)

No adoption papers were required back then. Far from it.

Welcoming a furry friend to its forever home took as much forethought as grabbing a pack of gum at the checkout. "Free" worked like magic, and it got people every time. (I am not immune to the ploy and admittedly once fell victim to a common gimmick known as "a complimentary lunch buffet." I now own a timeshare in Rhode Island. In fact, it might be all of Rhode Island.)

George named his rescue "Speedy" because he felt "it sounded strong." His strong hamster needed strength because he soon developed odd growths in his tail region. They were initially the size of Skittles, then morphed into Junior Mints, then elongated to Mike and Ikes. Eventually, when they expanded into marshmallow Circus Peanuts, Speedy busted right out of those skinny jeans. (Lumps are often described in terms of vegetables—pea size this or Brussels sprout that—but don't you agree that candy is a more universally understood concept?)

I dodged the medical issue as long as possible, but George quickly reminded me of the legally binding contract I had signed and insisted we seek professional care. I reflected on his own astronomical medical bills: his premature birth and hospitalization in the NICU; physical therapy for torticollis; a helmet for his misshapen head; five ear tube surgeries; eyeglasses *and* contact lenses; compacted molar removal; and two sets of braces. Two! (The term "million-dollar smile" must have been coined by a parent paying orthodontic bills.) Oh, I nearly forgot about the ER visit when he ran over his own hand with a skateboard—not his foot but his hand.

Instead, I opted to call a relative who's a true animal aficionado and explained that ~~we~~ George was worried about his beloved pet. She was kind and patient and asked a variety of questions. "Yes, there are two," I replied. "Yes, they are symmetrical … uh-huh … yes … toward his rear. Ohhhhhhh!"

The good news was that Speedy didn't have a tumor. The bad news was that his expansive testicles practically immobilized him, and he spent his days lounging on them like Truant Einstein on his gaming chair. We had to exchange his skinny jeans for a pair of MC Hammer pants and told George, "You can't touch this." Speedy's mobility suffered to the extent that we renamed him Molasses.

Surprisingly, he lived to 28 months (135 turtle years, 108 dog years). George was so hysterical at the news of his passing that Hank bolted home from a business dinner to provide comfort, obviously having listened to Harry Chapin's *Cat's in the Cradle* too many times. The following morning, I found Molasses in a velvet-lined hamster casket—my eyeglass case. With its lid up, he laid in repose next to the exercise wheel, a strand of white twinkle lights intertwined throughout the mesh. George looked handsome in his suit and clip-on tie. The entire neighborhood showed up to bid farewell as if it were a state funeral. One family sent an edible arrangement larger than the cage itself.

I recalled the deaths of our family's mutts, Tippy and Lassie. My mom and dad dragged their lifeless bodies across the backyard by their tails, leaving behind a path of smooshed grass. Then they wrapped them in black Hefty trash bags and unceremoniously buried them in the yard in unmarked graves. They were practically mobsters.

During Molasses's service I mulled over what to do with his remains. Under normal circumstances I wouldn't stow a pet inside a kitchen appliance, but die in February in the Midwest, and burial options are limited. (I keep preaching that our actions have consequences, but no one ever listens, Erma. No one *ever* listens.) I briefly considered, not as an act of retribution for croaking during an inconvenient time of year but for practical reasons, utilizing the garbage disposal or our pressure-assisted toilet. Ultimately, I decided it was an undignified rainbow bridge, even for a rescue rodent. I also worried that his overdeveloped manhood might clog either of them and I wasn't about to explain that to the Roto-Rooter man.

So, until spring thaw, he will rest in peace between a 1.5L Tupperware of leftover meatloaf and a bag of tater tots.

Hey, will you please do me a favor? Give me some sign or warning if there will be a power outage.

Yours truly,

Me

MIRROR MIRROR ON THE WALL, WHO'S THE VAINEST OF THEM ALL?

Dear Erma,

Aging has turned me into a human version of the Swiffer Sweeper Floor Mop Starter Kit—I can be wet and dry at the same time. On the bright side, perimenopausal nighttime sweating has permitted me to finally declare I am hot in bed. The negative part is that my skin has completely dried up, and my crow's feet have more lines than Leo Tolstoy's *War and Peace*. My stylist even diagnosed my hair with multiple personality disorder. Some strands lay flat while others stand and proudly sing the National Anthem (*Oh, gray can you see. . .*). When whiskers began sprouting from my chin like a Chia Pet, I had no choice but to invest in surgical tweezers from a medical device company. I justified the price because show me a woman whose beauty icon is Colonel Sanders.

My lowest point was when Hank discovered the tube of Replens in my nightstand drawer. "Do you use?" he asked. *Use.* As if I were a drug addict secretly injecting heroin in the space between my hammer toes.

But I have no right to complain because today there are noninvasive alternatives to living in such a primitive manner. With enough money, bravery, and patience waiting on hold to book an appointment, these issues can be nothing but a memory.

A vaginal rejuvenation expert can use Pinterest macrame techniques to return me to Slip 'N Slide condition. An injection specialist can stab my pores with poison-filled needles to decrease perspiration, leaving me only to pant like a dog anytime it's above 65 degrees. A laser technician can absorb my under-eye fat with a ShamWow! until transformed from slack hammocks into taut military beds with hospital corners (and since Bill served in the Army, I am certain he would appreciate that visual). An aesthetic nurse can even draw my blood, place it in a centrifuge to turn my plasma into a gated community by separating the rich from the poor, then inject the platelet-rich, posh stuff back into my scalp to grow healthier follicles. See how simple that was?

What I cannot fathom is why people choose to go under the knife if not "medically necessary," a term that has become wide open to interpretation. Some women consider it essential to reclaim their virginity—not by listening to Air Supply albums but by getting a hymenoplasty. Others feel a labiaplasty is necessary to return their oversized scrunchie to a mini scrunchie so they can once again dazzle their yoga class during half-moon pose. There are men convinced that turning their pesky outie belly buttons into innies through an umbilicoplasty will make their self-confidence soar to

Starlink heights. Most astounding is when people reshape their ears like an elf, file their teeth like a vampire, or augment their gluteals like travel neck-pillows. (No longer are implants exclusively cochlear, heart, or dental.) I swear, this is not fake news! (Just fake everything else.)

It would be hypocritical to claim that I am against all cosmetic surgery. Many women pray for large breasts, but mine caused tremendous pain and misery. (Psalms 23:5 suggests being grateful for a cup that runneth over but tell that to someone whose bra size extends into the LMNOP section of the alphabet.) I am still trying to overcome the humiliation suffered when George commented that they looked like gingerbread man legs.

So, I had a reduction mammoplasty. During the consultation, the surgeon used a grape-colored marker to draw geometry formulas all over my chest. It was as if *Harold and the Purple Crayon* was imagining a new world for my areoles. Aside from Olive Garden's Never Ending Pasta Pass, it's the best gift I've ever given myself. Admittedly, the eight-hour fasting period prior to anesthesia was torture but proved worthwhile when I was finally able to retire my push-up bras. For sixteen hours per day, those poor suckers took the exhaustive stance of the Marines raising the American flag at Iwo Jima.

In Japan, broken objects are often repaired with gold. The flaw is seen as a unique piece of the object's history and adds to its beauty. If Americans followed this custom, everyone would be walking around looking like C-3PO in the desert sun.

Erma, you once wrote, "According to my girth, I should be a ninety-foot redwood." Today you might be tempted to obtain the waistline of a sapling, although that doesn't seem like your style.

People like Goldilocks really do exist. Instead of criticizing food, furniture, and incorrect Sleep Number mattress settings, they harshly judge their bodies: "This is too big," and, "This is too small." If only it could be like in the storybook. Wouldn't it be refreshing to hear, "Ahhh, this is just right!"

Yours truly,

Me

EXTRACURRICULAR CHAOS

Dear Erma,

We have a three-car garage and nowhere to park my 2009 Kia Soul with 238,000 miles. Instead, it is a storage facility for kickballs, footballs, golf balls, croquet balls, juggling balls, bowling balls, Ping-Pong balls, tennis balls, racquetballs, volleyballs, lacrosse balls, basketballs, balls, beach balls, tether balls, and Hacky Sack balls. (Phillies Karen stole all our baseballs.) Listen to me. I sound like Bubba rattling on to Forrest Gump about the multitude of ways to prepare shrimp.

You might be curious how our collection got so enormous. I entirely blame the community education catalogs, school extracurricular pamphlets, and summer camp brochures crammed into our mailbox daily, each thicker than the LSAT prep book.

Oblivious to the cost, schedule, or location, George examines them with the thoroughness my sisters and I gave the Sears Christmas Wish Book. Using color-coded magic markers, he highlights anything of remote interest until the pages look like a television color-test pattern, disregarding course descriptions with the words *pony, sewing, nutrition, stewardship, and emotions*.

My mom learned of upcoming activities from the grocery

store bulletin board above the gumball machines. A couple times a year when something caught her eye, she jotted down the information on the back of her checkbook, and I soon found myself competing in a gunny sack race, learning to churn butter, or singing Judy Collins songs at a senior citizen luncheon. On good days we found the event happened three years ago but was still posted on the board, letting us leave without further embarrassment, though not without being asked to sing Judy Collins songs.

Always included in the fee is a ball and a T-shirt. Every year, without fail, I miscalculate George's size, and the shirt ends up hanging down past his ankles. Depending on the color, my poor son looks like the Pac-Man ghosts: Blinky, Pinky, Inky, or Clyde.

I suppose the expense and clutter are worth it because idle hands do the devil's work. When George asked, "If I twiddle my thumbs long and fast enough will the house set on fire?" it prompted me to enroll him in an activity that wouldn't increase our homeowner's insurance.

You once wrote, "I don't participate in any sport with ambulances at the bottom of the hill." Believe me, you wouldn't have had to worry about injuries with the lackluster gang enrolled in beginning soccer. On the first day of practice, after the coach handed the participants (a generous word, in this case) their balls and T-shirts, one stinker promptly parked his butt in the shade and entertained himself with his stupid fidget spinner. Another punk stole his mother's phone, camped out on the sidelines, and watched unboxing videos on YouTube. Her response to his laziness? "Way to stay hydrated, Sport!" *Ugh.*

George and the few remaining players performed drills. With their fists set firmly on their hips and their little feet hopping about, they looked more like Michael Flatley in *Riverdance* than Lionel Messi at Inter Miami CF.

A hulk wearing a tank top that read: MY FAVORITE SOCCER PLAYER CALLS ME DAD, shoved a snack sign-up sheet in my face and mansplained the only permitted items were hard-boiled eggs, nut-free granola bars, raw veggies with hummus, and mandarin oranges with encouraging messages written on the peel in non-toxic marker. I must have missed the *Sports Illustrated* article about the athlete perishing without caloric intake for thirty minutes. Begrudgingly, I signed up for early November and planned to bring leftover Halloween candy.

I've never claimed to know much about sports. In fact, the first time the coach hollered, "Nice D!" I assumed he was complimenting my boobs. But one thing I *have* noticed is that team names may not hint of aggression or violence. By today's standards, *The Wizard of Oz*'s Dorothy could not say one peep about lions, tigers, or bears. *Oh my!*

Only unobjectionable, universally loved things are allowed, which means fans now cheer on teams such as *Baby Giggles, Hedgehogs,* and *Towels Straight from the Dryer.* My nephew plays shortstop for the *Betty Whites.* Epic uniform, I must say.

For George's birthday, I asked what gift he might like to

receive. He asked for something simple, budget friendly, and a cinch to fulfill: a new ball. But Hank said, "Not so fast. Have you been in the garage lately?" I hadn't. Not since he began referring to it as the "man cave."

Instead of spending $3, he bought a $600 trampoline. George bounced on it for three minutes then sighed, "It sure would be fun to have a hoop attached. Then, of course, I'd need a new basketball."

Tomorrow, I have to wake up early to register Hank for a community education class titled, "How to Let Go of Your Balls." For his sake, I sure hope it's about decluttering the garage.

Yours truly,

Me

IT'S A PRIUS! IT'S A CYBERTRUCK! IT'S SUPER DAD!

Dear Erma,

Today I spent several thousand dollars paying for my car to get "some work done." I can't even afford my own midlife crisis. At least the waiting room had an assortment of snacks and a comfortable couch that Tom Cruise would have jumped on if given the chance. Initially I had the place to myself, but other customers soon trickled in.

First was a guy wearing a T-shirt that read: DAD: THE MAN, THE MYTH, THE LEGEND. His toddler looked like Houdini performing his underwater torture escape trying to free himself from his stroller. When his harness was unfastened, the miscreant smacked him in the face with a precision Moe, Larry, and Curly would have applauded. I winced, anticipating a spanking, but the father smiled and calmly said, "No, thank you, sweetie," as if declining a coffee refill at IHOP. Then, to make matters worse, the split-second the boy's strobe-light, roller-sneakers touched the floor, he screamed like I did upon learning NBC didn't renew *This Is Us*.

Erma, my dad would have encased the lower half of my face in duct tape if I had behaved in such a manner. But this progressive parent gently rubbed Lucifer's back and said, "Buddy, I understand you're experiencing big emotions right now but please use your words." Did that happen? No. The lad aimed his Nerf gun at Dad's crotch and pulled the trigger. "The man, the myth, the legend" collapsed on the floor and wailed, "Hands are for hugging!"

I was stunned. Never would I have expected such a young man to suffer from projectile dysfunction, particularly one who drove a four-door extended-cab pickup with truck nuts hanging from the hitch. Come to think of it, that might be where he put his.

Next to enter the lounge was a hipster dropping off his Prius equipped with eyelash extensions accentuating the headlights and a handlebar mustache decal on the grill. (The front end looked like the lovechild of Tammy Faye Bakker and the Pringles man.) His fuschia GIRL DAD cap was louder than his four mute daughters. To be fair, I cannot be certain they were mute, but in three hours not once did any of them glance away from their respective iPads. Instead, they stayed in their own little virtual worlds, pawing at their digital pacifiers in the way I always imagined Lenny from *Of Mice and Men* compulsively touched soft things. The "girl dad" often tried to give them fist bumps, but they ignored him, and his knuckles dangled uselessly from his wrist. Classic case of limpotence.

Erma, you once wrote, "Somewhere it is written that parents who are critical of other people's children and publicly admit they can do better are asking for it." That is precisely the reason I decided to insert another Snickerdoodle instead of my opinion.

Marching into the lounge next was a battalion and their leader carrying SUPERDADS DON'T BABYSIT totes overflowing with hand sanitizer, wooden labyrinth puzzles, kinetic sand, and homemade slime. After the army polished off their buffet of fresh fruit and vegetables, one of the little soldiers asked, "Sir, may I please have a cookie before that lady eats them all?"

Well, Dad sprung to his feet and yelled, "What do we say to temptation?" I couldn't have been more astonished when the troops stomped their feet on the floor. Half of them chanted, "WILL!" while the others cheered, "POWER!" This went on and on, over and over. "Will power, will power, will power!" My eyes played hot potato looking back and forth between them, my left brain chanting, *Quiet!* and my right brain cheering, *time! Quiet time, quiet time, quiet time!*

Just as the "superdad-who-doesn't-babysit" seemed satisfied, they swarmed the cookie tray and inhaled every last crumb. Embarrassed from such a public display of premature congratulations, he bellowed, "ATTENTION! BUG OUT!" and they fled in their Cybertruck newly equipped with fresh HEPA filters to restrict harmful agents from penetrating the cabin.

Erma, I absolutely support dads who assume an active role in parenting. It's a win/win for everyone involved: the co-parents, teachers, coaches, and future parole officers. My own dad sat in his La-Z-Boy recliner, leisurely watching *60 Minutes* and *M*A*S*H*, oblivious to my exhausted mother single-handedly performing 99% of the household tasks. An appropriate T-shirt for him would have included your quote, "When my kids become wild and unruly, I use a nice, safe playpen. When they're finished, I climb out."

No one needs clothing with clever sayings or vehicles with ridiculous accessories. Instead, some good, old-fashioned common sense would go a long way. And a platter of Snickerdoodles wouldn't hurt, either.

Yours truly,

Me

ACTUALLY, THERE IS FUN IN FUNERAL

Dear Erma,

It is my birthday. I'm at the age when time is no longer measured by the calendar but rather the level reached on my health insurance deductible. I celebrated by having my annual physical, which was akin to the 100,000-mile service recommendation mark on a car: oil change (PAP smear); rust-preventing coat (shingles vaccine); transmission fluid change (colonoscopy); battery analysis (EKG); timing belt replacement (hormone therapy); water pump (kidney function test), and a friction car wash (mammogram).

For me, the most uncomfortable part is the breast exam. I always worry Doc will think I'm attracted to him if my nipples get hard. On the other boob, if they don't respond at all I'm convinced it's a sign of terminal disease. Worst of all is when the right and left sides cannot agree on how to behave. Although accurately representative of our political parties, I'd like to think that one side of the room is simply warmer than the other, like two fronts setting up a winter squall that shuts down I-80.

When Doc asked if I had noticed any swelling, beads of

sweat formed on my brow, a chill went down my spine, my mouth went dry, and my mind went straight to the C-word—*copay*. I hadn't even met my maximum out-of-pocket!

Hank tried to assure me everything would be all right, insisting I was too stubborn to die. Still, I mentally began using my Groupons, canceling my plant identification subscription, and returning the 240-pack of coffee pods. More than anything else, I prayed I would die doing what I love—shopping at HomeGoods when an avalanche of My Pillows falls off the top shelf and lands on my head.

I also began to think about the type of funeral I wanted. When I visited your gravestone at Woodland Cemetery in Dayton, Ohio, I admired your lovely marker, memorial stone, and bench. I, too, considered going the traditional route. But I cringed imagining people peering into my casket and feeling dismayed that I never figured out how to find the right shade of foundation. (The whole "warm versus cool" thing confused me. I even bought the wrong type of humidifier.)

Briefly, I contemplated donating my body to science but then recalled my MRI report, which described me as a "well-nourished female with an unremarkable brain." It didn't seem fair that brilliant medical students would be stuck studying my mediocre cranial contents and develop carpal tunnel syndrome dissecting my thick layers of subcutaneous tissue.

Instead, I decided on cremation. Sure, its carbon footprint is significant, but why should Bill Gates and his private jet have all the fun? Additionally, it was far less expensive, which allowed room in the budget for a taco food truck luncheon after the church service.

Cremains can be infused with seeds, planted, and grown into a tree; dissolved into ink and used as a tattoo (I wonder if Jelly Roll has opted for this); disposed at sea by a company rumored to be owned by Robert Wagner and Christopher Walken; or stuffed into fireworks and blasted into the air. (Why only sing *On Eagle's Wings* when you can land on one?) The sky is literally the limit.

I decided to commission an Etsy artist to etch your famous words into my urn: "If I had my life to live over, I would have burned the pink candle sculpted like a rose before it melted in storage." (I hope you haven't wasted too much time on regrets, Erma. For all you know that candle could have smelled like Gwyneth Paltrow's vagina.)

As it turned out, my plans were premature. As I was composing my obituary, "In lieu of flowers, please ban pumpkin spice lattes prior to October 1st," Doc called with the results. "Good news! You are completely normal."

Erma, I laughed so hard that I almost died!

Yours truly,

Me

SUPPLE-MENTAL CASE

Dear Erma,

Stepping in to the pharmacy section of Walgreens this afternoon made me feel as lost as the time I ventured into Tokyo's Shibuya train station during rush hour without a pocket translator, trekking poles, or compass.

I was in search of a basic daily supplement but there were more options than books in the Library of Congress. Overwhelmed with the array of bottles of vitamin B1, B6, B7, and B12, I blurted out, "BINGO!" and approached the pharmacist for a prize. She directed me to a computer that launched a detailed questionnaire designed by an FBI profiler. I would answer one prompt, and another immediately popped up in its place.

> *What is your ultimate goal: to improve bone, liver, brain, heart, or mental health; weight loss; digestion; immunity support; general wellness; or something else? (fill in the blank).* My answer: To win the Powerball.
>
> *Do you prefer liquids or solids?* My answer: Liquids (particularly when the restroom is out of toilet paper).

Do you prefer sweetened or unsweetened? My answer: My dentist drives a Bugatti, what do you think?

What are some of your favorite flavors? Do you like cherry? Do you like peppermint? Do you like piña coladas and getting caught in the rain? …

Erma, the end appeared to be nowhere in sight. I was standing so long that my knees began to buckle, and I resorted to borrowing a cane from aisle 7's mobility aid section so I could finish without collapsing.

At last, the printer spat out 1,2,3 … 11 pages! I returned to aisle 7 to exchange the cane for a portable commode to rest on while I reviewed the report. A diagram looked like a family tree from *Sister Wives.*

It indicated I was a moderately overweight (true) middle-aged (true) woman (I believe so, but as *Daily Wire's* Matt Walsh asks, "What is a woman?"). It somehow even knew that I was able to separate the song "Baby, It's Cold Outside" from the #MeToo movement and enjoy it as a festive holiday tune. How it knew George's dead hamster was in the freezer is beyond me.

It suggested one product that would remediate all my flaws and quirks. For only $129 for a thirty-day supply with auto-renewal subscription, The Ideal Woman Elixir, which four out of ten doctors recommended, would turn me into Jessica Alba, although ***results not typical.

Many other "new-and-improved" products have made traditional ones obsolete. A greasy pizza used to cure a hangover, but now recovery and detox formula is preferred. Pepto-Bismol used to aid leaky guts and butts, but consumers now turn to probiotics, prebiotics, postbiotics, and when all else fails, flatulence-filtering clothing.

Hot washrags have been replaced with Boogie Wipes, and a glass of warm milk and a lullaby were ditched for lavender-scented melatonin pillow spray. Forget Band-Aids. A skinned knee is covered with a Bravery Badge as if a damn Purple Heart. All this nonsense makes me want to throw in the copper-infused towel.

As a kid, if I became ill, my mom put a pillow and blanket on the couch, set out a sick bucket next to a tray of dry toast and ginger ale, and let me convalesce while binge-watching game shows and soap operas. I may or not receive a St. Joseph aspirin for children.

What did you and Bill keep inside your medicine cabinet at 162 Cushwa Drive? Did you dab cotton balls of Calamine lotion on Betsy's mosquito bites? Massage Vick's VapoRub onto Andy's congested chest? Stick a mercury thermometer's cool, metal tip under Matt's tongue?

You once wrote, "It's frightening to wake up one morning and discover that while you were asleep you went out of style." But what is even more frightening is not waking up at all. Of course, the right vitamin can prevent dying altogether, although ***results not typical.

Yours truly,

Me

TINY HOUSE ON THE PRAIRIE

Dear Erma,

One thing I've learned about air travel is that when my assigned seat number comes close to matching my bra size, the flight is going to stink. Literally. Seat 38D is adjacent to the restroom, and an emergency oxygen mask is the only way to survive the biscotti break. (By the way, don't you find the word *restroom* a bit of a stretch? As if tucked under the diaper changing station is a king-sized Murphy bed available for weary passengers to take naps. Even the use of the word "room" is generous considering it is the size of a Little Free Library.) When Johnny Carson flew you to New York to appear on *The Tonight Show,* was your ticket first-class?

My biggest gripe is when the flight crew fails to extend the seatbelts to maximum length prior to boarding. It's so humiliating having to employ a half ton-rated ratchet strap to simply loosen my buckle. *Zzzzzip zzzzzip zzzzzip* echoes throughout the entire cabin, and I just want to hide in the overhead compartment, which doesn't even fit my fanny pack. It makes me wonder who sat there before me: the Travelocity gnome?

When Hank suggested just the two of us escape on a little getaway, I told him I didn't care what we did, where we went, or how long we stayed, as long as we traveled by car. And so, he decided we would go camping.

Now, anyone who claims roughing it is part of the fun has never slept on a leaky air mattress. Hank pumped it up more than a bike tire at the Tour de France, but it soon deflated, and we realized we built our campsite over the rockiest ground this side of the Badlands. If we had cell service, I would have notified the American Museum of Natural History that a Stegosaurus fossil was buried beneath my musty sleeping bag. (In retrospect, perhaps the title character in *Princess and the Pea* deserved compassion instead of being labeled "high maintenance.")

To make matters worse, our tent was constructed from the same material as incontinence products and absorbed every drop of moisture within a twenty-mile radius. The single, flap-down window provided little ventilation, and the interior temperature soared to that of a wood-fired pizza oven. In Hank's defense, I'm sure the gear was in better condition when he last used it in 1974 at Boy Scout Camp.

You once wrote that humor is "an outburst that just comes. It's unbridled, it's unplanned, it's full of surprises." The same could be said of mosquitos. One little fellow kept us awake the entire night practicing his audition for *The Voice.* He also drew enough blood from me—not Hank, of course—to land a role on *The Sopranos*.

This morning when I stood up, my spine sounded like a glow stick being activated. I decided to go for a walk to ~~stretch my legs~~ sulk. I was peering through the bird-watching binoculars when something caught my eye. Our neighbor's tiny house was posher than our actual home. A chandelier. Stainless steel appliances. An HVAC system operated by Greta Thunberg's line of solar panels. Shit, it even had a bidet.

What gave it a homey feel, though, was the décor: the faux moose head positioned above the faux fireplace, the faux leather couch, the faux fur blanket, and faux goose feather throw pillow. Even the patio's faux stone pavers resembled the yellow brick road on the way to the Land of Oz, the magical place where all wishes were guaranteed to come true. All you had to do was click the heels of your 1974 Boy Scout hiking boots three times.

I felt as if I were floating, the kind of out-of-body experience that survivors report in natural disaster documentaries. Instantly, I was tasered with the realization that our thirty-year mortgage was a total sham. You were right, Erma, "The grass is always greener over the septic tank," *and* the glamping tent.

When I groused that we didn't have a pot to piss in, Hank argued that we *did,* but it was currently being rinsed in the stream before we cooked the breakfast beans. *Breakfast beans? If that's what I wanted I'd have booked a red-eye to London and ordered the Full English.* Forget keeping up with the Kardashians, we couldn't keep up with the Ingalls. The Waltons would consider us a charity case.

If memory serves me correctly, I recognized the people as the winners of HGTV's *Most Stylish Dorm Room*. Can you believe such a silly competition exists? What was your style at the University of Dayton? My freshman college dorm could have passed for a mid-century prison cell. The only decoration was a poster of a fried egg in a cast-iron skillet serving as a reminder of how my brain would look on drugs. (It was also my brain in Psych 101 at eight o'clock in the morning, but that's a different story.) When I laid upon my three-inch-thick plastic mattress (four-inch, including the foam egg crate topper) I gazed up at two parallel fluorescent light bulbs that buzzed to the beat of *Footloose*. Everyone's rooms looked the same.

Anyway, when Hank and I returned home a few hours ago, we looked like the final castaways on *Survivo*r—exhausted, sunburnt, starving, and covered with scabs. I lost so much weight that if we had flown home instead of driven, the airplane seatbelt would have fit around my waist no problem and I would have been in a better seat because my bra size dropped to 32A—a window seat! (Take that, gingerbread man!)

Hank unpacked the car, and I paid some bills. I licked the stamps and sighed, knowing it was the closest I would ever come to first class.

Yours truly,

Me

MY WASHING MACHINE IS SMARTER THAN YOUR HONOR STUDENT

Dear Erma,

I'm jealous of my Roomba. Doesn't it sound dreamy to eat everything in your path, collapse, take a nap, then get carried back home?

Today it perished smack dab in the entryway. I tripped over the lazy thing, twisted my ankle, and sliced open my toe. "Low battery," it groaned. *Yeah, join the club! At least you got to eat first.*

I returned it to the docking station and heard uncontrollable laughter. The Ring camera had witnessed the entire event and shared the footage with her bestie, Alexa. (Those two are thick as thieves, Erma.) In her stern British accent, Alexa suggested I get LASIK eye surgery. I snipped back that the only thing I needed was a moment to get off the floor, and she quipped, "Denial ain't just a river in Egypt." She then loaded the directions to Africa on Waze. "Egypt is 6,843 miles as the crow flies. By the way, you have a severe case of resting bitch face."

Ha! They don't know me at all! My bitch face never rests!

I hobbled to the laundry room and threw my bloody sock into the washing machine. I've had that thing for three years and still cannot figure out how to use it. It took me a full minute to select the proper cycle due to the knob having more reference marks than a maritime clock. And by "proper cycle," I mean 10 black because I just let the knob spin like a roulette wheel.

I figured if the vacuum could take a break, then so could I (though the bitch face remained). I was desperate to dive into a juicy hardcover, but Kindle has replaced them all. So, I mindlessly clicked on the remote, which brought up a list of every cringey show I've ever watched. How has our country completely forgotten about former Congressman Anthony Weiner's wiener scandal, but my television will forever remind me of the twelve seconds I tuned in to *Here Comes Honey Boo Boo*? It's unnerving, Erma. That is *my* unintellectual property. Five minutes of channel flipping proved that every show had the intellectual depth of *Bridezillas*, so I gave up.

I limped to the kitchen and poured myself a "World's Okayest Mom" mug of boxed Chardonnay and was halfway back across the room when the fridge decided to join the conversation. "Door ajar . . . door ajar . . . door ajar . . . door ajar . . ." she harped on in a catty tone. I yelled "&@+?1(*#~$" but Alexa scolded, "Don't tell her to shut the duck up. Just get up and close the ducking door." Talk about sassy. My poor mom used to defrost our freezer manually, a chore that required five hours, a parka, ski gloves, goggles, a chisel, and the next day, a chiropractor. She never whined.

Anyway, the washing machine alerted me that my sock was clean with a buzz lasting longer than the 2023 SAG-AFTRA strike. It really should program more appealing sounds. For example, if it jingled like an ice cream truck, I might be more enthused to fold Hank's Fruit of the Looms.

Next thing I knew, my phone went berserk. First was a National Wireless Emergency Alert, then a weather app notification about an imminent ice storm, which caused the furnace to announce, "Overdrive heat activated," as if suffering from hot flashes.

You once wrote, "Some emotions don't make a lot of noise. It's hard to hear pride. Caring is real faint, like a heartbeat. And pure love, why some days it's so quiet, you don't even know it's there." I sure wish all these so-called smart appliances would take note; they speak to me more than my own family.

I decided to take a nap and had enjoyed a few hours of slumber when I was awoken by the Roomba chirping, "Battery is fully charged."

Pffft! I could only wish!

Yours truly,

Me

FROM TATER TOTS TO BENTO BOX – THE LUNCHROOM EVOLUTION

Dear Erma,

For the first time ever, I decided to surprise George by popping into his school for lunch. A team of TSA agents escorted me through the bulletproof sallyport, examined my ID, interrogated me over the purpose of my visit, guided me through a dual-energy X-ray machine, and inspected every last item in my purse. (They considered my extendable backscratcher a deadly weapon and confiscated it.)

George's class soon filtered into the cafeteria and unpacked spreads so artful I thought I had inadvertently stepped onto the set of *Top Chef.* Suddenly, I understood why Luigi Boccherini's *Minuetto* played on the loudspeaker.

One camper kiddo unveiled a s'mores kit along with a tabletop kerosene fire pit. A girl set out miniature blueberry heart pancakes that extended across the table. (Her lack of spatial awareness didn't get her suspended, but her vintage

Aunt Jemima pancake syrup bottle sure the hell did.) One little boy opened an actual tackle box with compartments overflowing with goldfish crackers, low-MSG sardines, dolphin-safe cocktail shrimp, seaweed snack sheets, and gummy worms for dessert. Another youngster plopped down a picnic basket, a gingham tablecloth, and a sprinkling of compostable toy ants. His twelve-course charcuterie board included ginger goat cheese and mock champagne in a BPA-free plastic flute.

When you wrote, "I come from a home where gravy is considered a beverage," was it made with sesame, turmeric, fig, date, pistachio, kelp, mango gelatin, and hemp milk? Those were the ingredients in the sauce a mini-Rachael Ray poured over her free-range, Thanksgiving-in-April turkey.

I asked what special occasions everyone was celebrating and was stunned to learn that such elaborateness was an everyday occurrence. George's pal, Hyphen Ampersand, was quick to provide a menu sample. Monday's theme was "mythical creatures," with julienne-sliced zucchini to emulate the Loch Ness monster's neck. On Tuesday, "iconic buildings around the world" showcased a giant heirloom portobello mushroom carved to resemble the Sydney Opera House. Today's "classic cartoon characters," however, was a massive failure. Although I instantly recognized the puréed pumpkin with black lentils as Fred Flintstone, no one knew who that was. Not even the teachers, who likely did not want to encourage ~~cave dweller Neanderthal~~ primal people of the Paleolithic thinking. (His parents are expected to file a motion with the USDA to reshape the food pyramid in the form of SpongeBob SquarePants.)

I would be remiss to mention the accessories: antibacterial and aromatherapy wipes; pre-meal and post-meal palate cleansers; and pre-cut strands of matcha green tea-flavored dental floss. And what kind of parent wouldn't include a DIY card touting an inspirational phrase such as, "You will conquer the world!" "I appreciate you!" and "You are magic!"

Sometimes a joke was also included. Roy G. Biv received this doozy today with his fruit and veggie kebabs made to look like Eric Carle's *The Very Hungry Caterpillar:*

> **Question:** What did Mary and Joseph say to Jesus after he forgot to turn off the lights and close the door?
>
> **Answer**: Were you born in a barn?
>
> **Today's lesson:** Do your part to conserve energy and save the planet!

Such an adorable way to prove lunacy runs in his bloodline.

When I was George's age, the entire school ate the same vague "mystery meat" and "chef's surprise" the hair-netted lunch lady shoveled onto our trays. My mom was far too busy to pack bagged lunches, but if she had, I am certain her note would have read, "Waste the crusts and don't bother coming home."

Anyway, I'm sure you can understand my reluctance to give George his lunch. I worried that the simple meal I packed would ignite an inferiority complex lasting decades. Nonetheless, he was famished so I handed over the sad sack and hung my head in shame.

For the first time in the school's history, the lunchroom became completely and utterly silent. I actually heard a marshmallow from the s'mores kit hit the floor. Curious voices soon crescendoed to a boom and crowds rushed our table like tween fans to Taylor Swift's stage.

"What's that?" someone cried out.

A collective gasp echoed when I replied, "A brown paper bag."

"And that?" a gal hollered, pointing to George's bologna sandwich with a chunk of Velveeta. Upon hearing my answer, she passed out cold. The school nurse revived her with smelling salts scented with sesame, turmeric, fig, date, pistachio, kelp, mango gelatin, and hemp milk.

By the time George bit into his saltine crackers slathered in lard, eleven pupils had suffered cardiac arrest. No one had an inkling that fruit grew as a whole piece and not in pre-packaged, dehydrated slices. They were today-years-old upon learning that popcorn came from corn kernels, not movie theater concession stands with leather recliners and a serving staff. Erma, I was like a modern-day Socrates introducing a generation of impressionable young minds to a new, old-fashioned world.

Tonight, I am going to sit by the fireplace and contemplate how I can continue to educate tomorrow's leaders. I might even roast a s'more.

Yours truly,

Me

SPANX FOR YOUR SUPPORT

Dear Erma,

George's level of honesty makes Mother Teresa look like Bernie Madoff. When my boy was still in the Pull-Ups stage, he meandered into my closet one morning as I was getting dressed, poked his index finger into my belly as if I were the Pillsbury Doughboy, and said, "Freeze the fat away with CoolSculpting!" (Unlike the Pillsbury Doughboy, I did not giggle.)

My muffin top captivated George. "It's like a double-decker bus!" he exclaimed, "ONLY BIGGER! Because a double-decker bus has two levels, and your tummy has three!" (For the first time in my life, I was an overachiever.)

Also, for the first time, I felt buyer's remorse for the eighteen months invested in his speech-therapy sessions. Why do you suppose mutism is considered a disorder requiring intervention when any mother can tell you it's a blessing equal to feeding the poor of Calcutta?

Although brutal, his truthfulness was the kick in the elastic-waisted pants I needed. Back when I was a high-school cheerleader and our captain, Tracy, effervescent as Pop Rocks shaken into a bottle of Coke, chanted, "Hands on hips, smile on lips," I happily obliged. I had no hips. I had no figure whatsoever. My butt was as white and flat as a cone coffee filter. I stayed thin for many years, incentivized by my ex-boyfriend's employment with the police force and his access to my driver's license photo. It was bad enough that he could see my address—proof that I traded my trendy urban loft for a mass-produced, gray house in the suburbs and I didn't want to further his poor opinion of me.

Fast-forward several decades, and my body has morphed into a more rotund version of its former self. Baroque artist Rubens would have felt compelled to retire his paintbrush had I been his muse. When my jowls filled out their change-of-address forms and permanently moved south, I prayed to the Patron Saint of Cellulite for mercy. Unfortunately, my fat rolls had become my not-hot-cross buns to bear. I blame Dot's Pretzels. And DOTS gumdrops. And my friend, Dot, a terrible influence in general.

Admittedly, Erma, I hate working out. My idea of exercise is running my mouth. The only time I run is if I *have* the runs. I lie around so much that I have been mistaken for a Life Alert actor, only I'm not asking to get back up. However, the day came when I realized I needed to change my ways. You would be proud of me, Erma. Right after my second breakfast dessert, I began fasting—the trendy, masochistic, self-flagellating phenomenon of willing starvation. However, on day #2, a terrifying sound made me bolt upright from a sound sleep. I feared it was a tornado because it is common knowledge they sound like an approaching freight train.

"Wake up," I hissed to Hank. "Something's wrong. I can feel it in my stomach." Well, he flopped over, pulled the duvet over his head, and moaned, "That *was* your stomach."

When you wrote, "I'm not a glutton—I'm an explorer of food," I considered alternative paths that might yield better results. I tried a liquid diet but that only added ten pounds. (It really should have clarified that chocolate malts were not allowed.) I followed an article's suggestion to eat the rainbow and saturate my plate with every hue on the color wheel, but I felt guilty over the wasted brown M&Ms. Another suggested veganism, but when it specified that even reading *Chicken Soup for the Soul* went against the philosophy, I knew it was too hardcore for me. (Truly, it was all for the best. Avocado toast looks exactly like a bear had, in fact, shit in the woods.)

During such trying times, I turn to an unconditional friend who lets me cry into her warm, tan shoulders and accepts me exactly the way I am. You had Mayva; I have Marie Callender. Marie convinced me to quit dieting altogether and instead purchase shapewear. It would magically revamp my silhouette from Mrs. Butterworth to Mrs. North Central Regional Midwest. Her advice sounded appealing, so I called my credit card company to increase my spending limit to the annual budget of Guatemala and ventured out to the department store.

When I was a young girl, I remember the undergarment section being nothing more than a plexiglass shelf displaying bras in cardboard boxes and pantyhose in plastic eggs. Therefore, I was shocked to see the overabundance of options. It was the beige fabric equivalent of the self-improvement section of a New Age bookstore in San Fransisco.

My whole life, I believed that I didn't want to *have* a great figure, I wanted to *be* one. No more. Fantasizing about my new shape was exhilarating! My arms would no longer look like soggy Brioche rolls. My kneecaps would bear no resemblance to Reynolds Wrap after falling from my hands, rolling across my grubby kitchen floor, and reversed back onto the cardboard cylinder.

I filled my cart as if a contestant on *Supermarket Sweep* with calf-Koozies (A.K.A. compression socks) and a miraculous skirted-swimsuit designed for modesty purposes by Sisters at the Most Blessed Sacrament Convent. I spotted a waist-cincher that, with such extreme pressure at the hooks and eyes, would become like launching rivets on the hatchways on the sinking *Titanic*. I was going to look sensational, damn it. (Speaking of, you should bear some of the responsibility here, Erma. After all, I got into this situation in the first place because you urged, "Seize the moment. Remember all those women on the *Titanic* who waved off the dessert cart.")

When I came across the Spanx rack, I reached for my purse magnifying glass, because this torso tourniquet had the approximate square footage of a Starburst wrapper. (Like you wrote, "Sometimes I can't figure designers out. It's as if they flunked human anatomy.") Even with the size 5X, it was a challenge to hoist it up. When I finally did, my midsection took the form of an atomic mushroom cloud.

This is absurd, I thought. *Me, a women's studies minor in college, going to such lengths (and widths)! Screw this and the stupid body-positivity sticker on the mirror.* Not all heroes wear body contour tape, Erma.

But this is the mortifying part—it wouldn't come off. The Band-Aid jingle sprung to mind: *I am stuck in Spanx-Aid and Spanx-Aid's stuck on me.* I. Could. Not. Move. I huffed and puffed and nearly blew the door down. I farted. I had heart palpitations. I dry heaved. I looked exactly like Hank watching the *Barbie* movie.

Although *Magic Mike* made it seem like ripping off clothes is sexy, retail stores frown upon it. So, I tried a few tricky stunts learned from watching George in parkour. Two palm spins, a cat grab, a kong vault, and a drop landing later, those Spanx came off me inch by inch until it was a heap at my feet. Red-faced from exertion and humiliation, I fled the dressing room like the cherry-flavored Kool-Aid man barging through a brick wall.

That night when I tucked my barb-tongued son into bed and he snuggled close, I braced for another insult. I told myself that I would accept his blows like a champ—a heavyweight champ—but a champ, nonetheless. But guess what he said? "Mommy, I love you more than every grain of sand on every beach in the whole world." *Ahhh, the speech therapy finally paid off!* Good or bad, words carry enormous weight, don't they?

Well, I must go. Marie invited me to dinner. Turkey potpie followed by Razzleberry pie. Yum! And if George pays me another compliment like that, I'll let him join me (and hope he never shuts his piehole again!).

Yours truly,

Me

CELEBRATE GOOD TIMES (OH, COME ON!)

Dear Erma,

Several weeks ago, a mysterious man showed up at our front door and handed me an envelope. I know what you're thinking, but thankfully, I was not being served divorce papers. (For years Hank warned there would be consequences for leaving the room without turning off the lights, but I assumed he only meant high electricity bills.)

The gentleman wore white gloves, which I had never seen anyone do except for *Downton Abbey* butlers, the brawny chaps who delivered my microfiber sofa, and a singular bottle of beer on the brewery conveyer belt on *Laverne & Shirley.*

I opened the silk-lined, wax-embossed envelope with calligraphy that rivaled the U.S. Constitution. Inside was an invitation embedded with gold flakes normally seen floating in Goldschläger bottles. "Please help us celebrate Calif's 1st birthday." What an unusual name! I expected Mary Poppins to appear and sing, "superCALIFragilisticexpialidocious, even though the sound of it is something quite atrocious," which would be perfectly on point.

Secondly, I had no clue how my family was connected to these people. We were more likely to be spotted in "The People of

Walmart" than at a venue mentioned in a magazine's "Best of" edition. And that, Erma, is precisely why we RSVPd for three.

The day of the party I was hesitant to hand my key ring to the complimentary valet. Not because he might steal my jalopy, but what about my emergency ChapStick, the quarter for my Aldi shopping cart, or the overdue library book titled *What's Your Poo Telling You?*

The grand parlor was decorated as I imagined one of JLo's many past and future weddings. Frida Kahlo's grave on Day of the Dead wasn't adorned with as many flowers. Michelangelo's "David" ice sculpture nearly touched the ceiling, and the water fountain was so massive I expected to find the *Friends* cast dancing in it.

White-gloved waiters scurried over to us with silver serving platters with various hors d'oeuvres and beverages. You once wrote, "In general, my children refuse to eat anything that hasn't danced on television." George is the same, so he passed on Paula Deen's White Bean with White Pepper and White Rice appetizer. However, he thoroughly enjoyed the concoction made by the Cookie Kingpin, a colleague of the Cake Boss.

A woman in a stunning Stella McCartney cocktail dress introduced herself as the hostess and pointed George toward the entertainment. He had the option of attending Bindi Irwin's traveling petting zoo, Jason Momoa's necklace-making class, or the mobile Willy Wonka and the Chocolate

Factory. Hank and I were handed a tablet and forced to sign a waiver of liability.

George's birthday celebrations are far tamer. He's thrilled to simply choose where to have dinner, and for the past three years has wandered around Sam's Club collecting food samples. My parents celebrated our birthdays at home with frozen pizza, Jolly Good soda, and a cherry chip Duncan Hines cake served right in the metal pan. Presents were small and inexpensive, things that today would be considered stocking stuffers: soda-flavored lip gloss, smelly stickers, or a deck of novelty cards. (I should have kept those. The exact Old Maid set I once owned is currently listed on Marketplace for $225.)

Hank and I tried tracking down Calif all night but eventually gave up. The hostess, who had changed into a sparkly Alexander McQueen evening gown, informed us that the special boy was actually in the Maldives with his day nanny, overnight nanny, and weekend nanny.

On our way out, the event planner, who had managed the inaugural balls of the past six presidents, handed *us* a gift bag the size of Scarlett O'Hara's green curtain dress in *Gone with the Wind*. (I will give credit where credit is due; she did a phenomenal job with the party. Like you once wrote, "When I stand before God at the end of my life, I would hope that I would not have a single bit of talent left and could say, 'I used everything you gave me.'" She can honestly say she gave it her all.)

Last weekend she had orchestrated a gender-reveal party which was equally as monumental. She coaxed Otis Williams, the only surviving member of the original Temptations, out of retirement to perform their hit song, "My Girl;" she set up games called "Stashes or Lashes?" and "Bow or Bowtie?" the prizes being precious stones and jewels. (I wonder what it would be like to own a gold crown instead of composite resin. Once I finish paying off my root canal, I might ask my endodontist with the penguin wrist tattoo about that.)

The fireworks show went awry and ignited a wildfire which burned ten thousand acres of forestland to the ground. However, the guests were quick to remark how the hazy, smoldering, pastel sky coordinated beautifully with the pink and blue cake pops.

The ultimate gender-reveal, of course, was in the Bible when Angel Gabriel descended from heaven and appeared before the Virgin Mary to declare, "You will conceive a son." Amateurs.

One night at the dinner table, when I was about seven years old, my mom plopped creamed corn next to a bowl of alphabet soup and said, "We're expecting." My brother was born at home without so much as a birth announcement in the newspaper. Back then the general assumption was that a pregnancy had come full-term when the mother stopped wearing maternity clothes and started carrying an infant.

Anyway, it shouldn't be surprising, but Hank, George, and I never did receive a thank you note for our gift to Calif.

Perhaps he didn't appreciate the finger puppets I had knit myself. In retrospect, I'm glad I only gave him six. An ingrate like that doesn't deserve a full set of ten.

I only saw the hostess one more time, standing ahead of me in line at the grocery store checkout. On the conveyor were her Dubai chocolates, hybrid roses, Ideal Woman Elixir, and French cheese sold by the ounce. I set down the divider between us, a symbol of many, many things, and unloaded my items. Hamburger Helper's white-gloved hand on the box seemed to be waving right at me.

Yours truly,

Me

HOW MUCH IS THAT SCHNOODLE IN THE WINDOW?

Dear Erma,

I thought it would be fun to start off with a quiz. Is NoScoDoToXoLo (1) a new *Star Wars* character; (2) the name of Elon Musk's latest tax write-off; (3) the presidential nuclear launch code or; (4) a genetically modified Nova Scotia Duck Tolling Retriever/Xoloitzcuintli mix?

Number 4 is correct. Designer dogs now rule the bark park. Essentially, they are the woof-woof version of a hotdish—a crazy concoction of random ingredients, minus the cream of mushroom/celery/chicken/broccoli/potato/onion soup.

You once wrote, "Cats invented self-esteem," but imagine the inflated ego on the purebred golden-haired Tibetan mastiff purchased for $2 million. I have blown more money on extra *Candy Crush* moves over the years, so far be it from me to judge how others spend theirs, but that pooch was a worse investment than FTX cryptocurrency exchange. And at least I rewarded my *Candy Crush* success with real candy afterward.

I can just imagine how one orders a custom canine. "I'd like an Irish Wolfhound with a side of Affenpinscher, hold the American pit bull terrier, an extra heap of Pembroke Welsh corgi, and a dollop of Portuguese water dog. Also, please be sure he has a hypoallergenic coat, an affinity for baths, blow dryers, fireworks, and turds that smell like a new car. As for size, I'll take the micro-mini-dwarf-teacup." (How do you surmise that's accomplished? Are they placed on a nonstick sheet and baked for three minutes at 325 degrees like Shrinky Dinks?) Most importantly, and this should go without saying, he must resist smelling crotches, particularly Russell Brand's.

As you can guess, Erma, these pampered pups literally live in the lap of luxury. After a doggie doula helps deliver the litter, the breeder posts their profiles on Plenty of Bitch. Their adoptions are celebrated with peanut butter cakes from the local barkery, brain teaser toys, CBD oils promising to alleviate sexual frustration, and DNA kits to study their complex heritage.

Our town recently excavated the historic cemetery and razed the mausoleum to erect a facility with far more importance—a doggie daycare. Now, premium pooches are able to enjoy climate-controlled suites boasting adjustable-height beds with aloe-infused distemper-pedic mattresses. "Therapissed" sessions focus on optimal intellectual, mental, physical, and social health, while SIT prep courses teach how to walk elegantly in designer Pupcci and Louis Mutton stilettos. (I should attend that lesson myself. I can barely climb stairs in Dansko clogs.)

Erma, where I grew up, all pets lived outdoors. Tippie and Lassie spent their summers chasing tractors, swimming in ponds covered with algae blooms, and amassing so many burrs in their fur we thought they had been attacked by porcupines (sometimes they suffered both). In cold months, they kept warm with a bale of hay and their God-given winter coat (not monogrammed from L.L. Bean). The rare times we went on vacation, we left them a sack of Alpo and a five-gallon bucket of water. By today's standards, Sarah McLachlan would be singing *In the Arms of the Angels* while ASPCA stormed the porch.

Come to think of it, dogs are never named Lassie anymore. The same goes for Shadow, Spot, or Patches. Modern fur babies have normal names that human newborns are rarely blessed with: Grace, Bella, Lucy, Oscar, and Max. If you found a rabies tag lying on the sidewalk you might assume a Disney cast member lost his ID badge. "Sam from Orlando," it might read. When I overheard someone discussing a crabby old lady named Sophia, I assumed she was referring to *The Golden Girls,* not a hangry chow-chow-hua-hua.

Historically, Best in Show at the Westminster Kennel Club sounded like members of the royal family. In 1929, the title went to Collie Laund Loyalty of Bellhaven; in 1964, Whippet Courtenay Fleetfoot of Pennyworth earned bragging rights; and in 1975 an Old English Sheepdog named Sir Lancelot of Barvan received the trophy.

I wonder what the winner's moniker will be in another decade when the competition is open to anything that identifies as a canine—perhaps a meerkat named Lou Lou Lemon of Los Angeles. Author W. Bruce Cameron will draft a novel inspired by true events, and it will be a *New York Times* bestseller, just you wait and see.

Yours truly,

Me

PRINCESS HAIRY

Dear Erma,

I started babysitting at twelve, the same age Paul Rudd stopped aging. My first clients' house was covered with religious paraphernalia, such as light switches that read JESUS LIGHTS UP OUR LIVES. (The months they paid their electricity bill I was able to see Jesus in action.)

Given their décor, you can imagine how flabbergasted I was to discover their stack of *Playboy* and *Playgirl* magazines in plain sight atop the fuzzy toilet tank cover. Every Friday night after changing the cherub's cloth diaper and putting him to bed, I locked myself in the bathroom, lit incense, listened to their Columbia House music club tape collection, ate Jiffy Pop, and dissected every page cover to cover. (It was basically a dress rehearsal for my life today except I now prefer to read *1001 Things to See Before My Bud Light Stock Value Dies.)*

Slacking off was justified, I told myself, because they paid a measley $.75 per hour and gave it to me in loose change. (I always wondered if the couple was out robbing laundromats, juke boxes, and arcades instead of going to bowling league.)

I found the inordinate amount of hair all over the models' bodies riveting. I had never seen a naked person except for a snapshot of my home birth, which appeared as if a bloody, seven-pound pilar cyst was being extracted from Weird Al Yankovic's scalp. My grandmother's wedding portrait was equally egregious. In her knee-length, white business suit, she looked as if she were interviewing for a job at Wells Fargo—in Siberia.

Times sure have changed. It has become socially acceptable for humans to have hair on our heads only. How the trace evidence technicians on *CSI: Crime Scene Investigation, CSI: Miami, CSI: NY,* and *CSI: Vegas* stay employed is anyone's guess. If you're attracted to hairy men, your choices are limited to gazing at Rudolph Zallinger's *March of Progress* illustration or tuning in to reruns of *Magnum P.I.*

I tired of the whole shaving —> depilatory —> waxing —> dermaplaning —> laser rigamarole and quit outright. One day, Ringling Brothers Circus sent me a LinkedIn invitation for their upcoming bearded lady auditions, so I thought it might be best to try electrolysis before they nominated me for the part of wolf-boy.

At the clinic, I was greeted by a technician whose Groucho Marx eyebrows were darker and thicker than my grandma's leg hair. Her white lab coat suggested she had just completed her shift at the Clinique counter, Chef Boyardee, or a psychiatric ward. Although I was there to deal with my chin hairs, she insisted on taking a peek at my ~~bikini~~ granny panty line.

Before I knew it, I found myself supine with my feet in metal stirrups, giving me flashbacks of George's birth when I pooped on the delivery table. You once wrote, "Laugh now, cry later," but tell that to someone whose thighs are spread apart like a Butterball turkey.

I had hoped to zone out to Delilah on iHeartRadio, but Groucho Marx wouldn't stop jibber-jabbering about my goals. Who did she think she was, my life coach? Nonetheless, I confided that I've always dreamed of meeting the royal family and have even practiced my curtsy at the off-chance I would run into Will and Kate at Hobby Lobby or a Coinstar kiosk.

"I meant your FUPA goals," she huffed. (Don't feel bad, Erma. I had to look up the definition too. FYI, Anna Lefler's book, *CHICK-tionary,* is *the* go-to resource on such subjects.) What statement did I want my pubic hair to express? A specific emoji? Peace symbol? Hogwarts insignia? The leg lamp from *A Christmas Story*? A fast-food logo? (Apparently, Melania Trump's marital contract requires she has McDonald's golden arches.)

At the very first zap, I insisted she stop. If I wanted to die by electrocution, I'd jaywalk in the state of Texas. However, she kept going until I threatened to report her to PETA.

What a humiliating experience! Why do you suppose I put myself in such a vulnerable, undignified position? For what benefit? Whose? Ward never complained about June Cleaver's beaver, nor has Hank about mine, so why the obsession?

The more I think about it, maybe Mom, Grandma, and midcentury models had it all figured out. Please tell Audrey Hepburn not to even *think* about threading her eyebrows. Is she just as beautiful in person?

Yours truly,

Me

NO MORE PENCILS, NO MORE BOOKS, NO MORE TEACHERS WITH SPINSTER LOOKS

Dear Erma,

Self-checkout aisle security screens were invented by sadists. As I scan my items, I tell myself: *don'tlookupdon'tlookupdon'tlookup,* but of course I do look up only to find Zelda from *Pet Sematary* staring back at me. If I was looking for insults, I'd have booked a table at Dick's Last Resort. (Unlike Sydney Sweeney, I don't have good genes.)

My self-esteem took another uppercut to the chins when I met George's teacher at school conferences this evening. Her name was Claire, and that is exactly what the students called her. I considered the informality unprofessional, but I suppose it's only natural to be casual with someone who wears a messy bun and leggings as pants.

My elementary teachers all looked like Ma Berenstain Bear in her polka-dotted dress, bonnet, pantyhose, and wicker picnic basket/purse. Claire, however, belonged on the runway at the Victoria's Secret Fashion Show. I bet she goes to the self-checkout just for fun.

Teachers aren't the only thing that has changed. When I

walked into the classroom, I felt as if I had landed on another planet. (But not Pluto, which is no longer categorized as one. How mortifying to be dumped on account of his small size and the entire cosmic world knowing about it.) For starters, there are alternatives to boring desks and chairs. To alleviate the wiggles during lessons, youngsters are free to cycle on Pelotons or bounce on gigantic purple sensory balls. (They reminded me of my hemorrhoids. Sometimes when I'm constipated I sing, "She'll Be Coming 'Round the Mountain When She Comes," another John Denver classic.)

When students feel overstimulated, they are welcome to chillax to the "calm corner," an oxygen capsule equipped with a zero-gravity tub. And when they need a break from SMART-boards and Chromebooks, the therapy dog, Namaste, is there to lend a willing paw. Namaste was a rescue.

Call me nostalgic, but I'm sad George's nose hairs won't get singed from the overhead projector's electric burn stench. He won't have the thrill of cleaning chalkboard erasers by clapping them together, then develop COPD from inhaling white dust particles. He will never learn to write in cursive. And he will be robbed of the joy of spinning a globe on its axis, then slowing it down by gliding his fingertips over the textured, raised-relief topographical areas. (The cellulite on my saddlebags resembles the stretch from Colombia to Argentina, but I won't force him to touch it for the sake of education.) He is missing so much.

As if I didn't hate math enough, I learned that I have been doing it wrong my whole life. Adding 1 + 1 is a twelve-step program normally seen in AA, which is ironic because the new math is driving parents to drink. And I do not care what Claire says, "carry the six" means leaving a bakery with a half-dozen Long Johns. She even teaches multiplication on a horizontal line instead of a vertical column, a technique that has led George to believe he can solve life's problems by lying down instead of standing upright.

Even grading systems have completely changed. Instead of A, B, C, D, and F, report cards share "respect, redirect, and reflect" remarks, which detail only positive things about the ~~little hellions~~ promising scholars. To view them, parents must log in to the school portal (first going through multiple steps to prove we are not robots).

I can just imagine you hauling a pile of textbooks and a lunchbox in your arms on your way to Emerson Junior High School and Parker Vocational High School. No one owned a backpack back then. Now gear can withstand a Mount Everest expedition or deployment to the Middle East. They come equipped with crossflow air-ventilation systems, hydration reservoirs, and shoulder straps thicker than a memory foam mattress. All that to carry absolutely nothing inside. The durable fabric, however, is needed to physically support their massive keychain collections dangling from carabiners. When I saw the backpacks lined up on hooks in the hallway, I feared the walls could collapse at any moment and prayed the school district had contracted a qualified structural engineer. Rome's Ponte Milvio Bridge, where tourists famously leave locks as a symbol of their everlasting love, doesn't display as much shimmering metal. I briefly mistook it for the lighting on the

Saturday Night Fever soundstage.

You once wrote, "As a child, my number one best friend was the librarian in my grade school. I actually believed all those books belonged to her." Same. Using the card catalog to find Beverly Cleary's latest release was the highlight of my week. But you don't need a librarian if you have no library. 1) Too many books have become banned; and 2) Screen time *is* the new library. Erma, you would just weep into Namaste's hypoallergenic coat.

Even the medical wing looked as if had been on *Extreme Makeover: School Edition*. It showcased a dozen beds with wrought-iron headboards and crisp white linens—very Williams Sonoma meets *Madeline*'s bedroom suite of her Parisian boarding school. I know this because, trust me, George is in there a lot. (Do you consider a root-beer craving a medical emergency? Debatable.) The school policy dictates the nurse must notify parents for every minuscule issue (but only if the "patient" first signs a HIPPA release form allowing access, and then again, we must prove we are not robots).

When I was in first grade and broke out with chicken pox, the principal ushered me into the janitor's closet, created a makeshift cot from stacked boxes of WD-40, and gave me blue packing peanuts to play with until 3 o'clock dismissal. Most of them ended up in my hair and I stepped off the bus looking like Marge Simpson.

Upon returning home tonight, George asked for help with his math homework. We were going around in circles (or hexagons or scalene triangles—I don't understand geometry either) until I cried out, "I feel like such a moron!" My sweet boy patted my shoulder and said, "But so many people love you!"

What a great answer! If Claire gave letter grades out, he would have scored an A+.

Yours truly,

Me

TRIGGER WARNING! THE FOLLOWING MESSAGES MAY INDUCE EYE ROLLS

Dear Erma,

I assumed World War III had arrived, or a high-level assassination had occurred, when I turned on the television this morning to see this message: **WARNING! THE FOLLOWING PROGRAM CONTAINS VIOLENCE, NUDITY, SMOKING, FOUL LANGUAGE, AND GRAPHIC IMAGES**. I perched on the edge of the couch, inhaled deeply, began to pray, and waited for what was to come. I expected to see something truly horrific, worse than photos of Tori Spelling living in an RV park, but it was only a projectile-squirting cyst on *Dr. Pimplepopper*.

Movies are often prefaced with similar disclaimers stating: "This film may contain outdated attitudes, language, and cultural depictions which some viewers may find disturbing or offensive." As a personal favor, will you please form a protective shell around my childhood photo albums? I shudder to think of the public outcry if ever exposed.

1978's Volume IV, page 14 shows Polaroids of Mom breastfeeding my four-year-old sister while Dad is drinking a can of Pabst Blue Ribbon and driving the rider lawn-mower with my toddler brother on his lap. (On page 19, bro is chugging the Pabst). On page 22, I am dipping my index finger into my Great Aunt Maude's brownie batter, and she is striking my knuckles with a wooden mixing spoon. Page 28 showcases Halloween costumes that today would result in meeting with a human resource manager.

If disclaimers are used for every trivial thing, don't you predict people will dismiss all of them? The Surgeon General will be the boy who cried wolf and before we know it, pregnant women will freely down Skinny Girl margaritas, blissfully unaware they will soon give birth to a warthog.

What *does* need a warning label is George's artwork. For Mother's Day he painted a picture of me using temperas named "jaundice," "meth rash," and "bruise." (On the bright side, he has a promising career as a Claude Monet counterfeit artist duplicating the *Water Lilies* series.) Using clay as a medium was no more flattering. A sculpture made in my likeness featured an electrical outlet nose, one crossed eye, hair like Clark Griswold's tangled clump of Christmas lights, and a body the shape of a Tylenol PM capsule. (Wilson from *Cast Away*, even toward the end of the movie when he floated away from the dilapidated raft, was more attractive.) On his latest pencil sketch, my complexion resembled a QR code. One scan took you to a BOGO sale on

Revlon Colorstay. I had so many chins my neck resembled a Jenga tower on the verge of collapse. Hunter Biden could have done better. You once wrote, "There is a thin line that separates laughter and pain, comedy and tragedy, humor and hurt." In this case, my lips and sparse eyebrows *were* the thin lines. They looked like Twiggy on Ozempic.

Had these masterpieces come with adequate notice, I may have been prepared. But that is not how it works. Without warning, we might witness a self-driving Tesla crash in the next lane or a teen choking on a Tide pod. We aren't able to press the pause/fast-forward/stop/rewind button on life's remote control.

When I reflect on how different things were fifty years ago, I remind myself they were also different just yesterday. The older I get, the faster the world is spinning, spinning, spinning at such a rate that (**WARNING!**) I might just die.

Yours truly,

Me

FOODIES GONE WILD

Dear Erma,

I have officially become the adult version of Mikey, the Life Cereal kid. Instead of discarding the blue cheese that's not supposed to be blue, I overheard George say, "Leave it for Mom. She'll eat it. She eats anything."

Mikey deserves heaps of credit. His own flesh and blood treated him like a human garbage disposal, but he shamelessly chomped away with the utmost dignity. As far as I'm concerned, he should be giving TED Talks on self-acceptance. National hero if you ask me.

I have never understood picky eaters. Sure, it's perfectly normal to have preferences and aversions. Everyone does. But there exists an altogether other realm rooted from never having experienced profound hunger. For instance, take Meg Ryan's character in *When Harry Met Sally*. Talk about fussy! The movie *should* have been titled, *Why Harry Ghosted Sally*.

Vegetarians have become extinct, vegans are endangered, and trendier subspecies have emerged. Pescatarians eat mainly fish. Beegans consume honey but exclude all other animal products. Lacto-ovo vegans eat animal products such as eggs, dairy, and fresh roadkill but only if slaughter is not involved. (Dairy Queen is currently conducting market research for their next Blizzard flavor. It has been reported that armadillos, although readily available in southern states, have proven not to be blender friendly.)

Other diets include Paleo, Keto, Raw, Mediterranean, High Fiber, Low Sodium, Low Carb, Low Calorie, Anti-Inflammatory, Soup, Smoothie, Blood Type, Body Type, Neuro, and others that will be invented by the time I finish writing this letter. Oh, I forgot to mention the lesser-known Dukan Diet, which initially skyrocketed in popularity due to mass confusion over the similar sounding Dunkin' Donuts Diet. I tried that last year and succeeded in gaining eighteen pounds. "Munchkins" does not mean smaller portions.

Then there is a phenomenon called "intermittent fasting," which isn't a diet at all, but something known as:

> "My-goal-is-to-appear-disciplined-and-self-righteous-when-in-reality-nothing-in-front-of-me-at-this-exact-moment-looks-appealing-but-just-you-wait-until-later."

And sit tight. Rice is now made from chickpeas, pasta from quinoa, and pizza crust from cauliflower. Talk about reinventing the Pampered Chef salad spinner! Perusing a restaurant menu takes forever because it is riddled with distracting asterisks that look like the Artist Formerly

Known as Prince symbol. In addition to indicating Kosher and Halal, it warns of exposure to gluten, tree nut, food dyes, shellfish, eggs, or other allergens. The cross-contamination is known as six degrees of Kevin Uncured Bacon.

Personally, I think having celiac disease would be the absolute worst. Imagine your only candy options being Peeps marshmallows and even more revolting, marshmallow Circus Peanuts. Ask Molasses; they're a drag.

The common term in all these lifestyle choices is "organic." Even water! *WATER*. Rust, too, is organic, which I learned when George's pediatrician chided me for allowing him to drink from a rusty garden hose before his first tetanus shot.

The philosophy "farm to table" is frequently used as well, although I more often practice "drive-thru to lap." Particularly amusing to me is the expression "clean eating," as if the regular groceries I buy are unsanitary, filthy trash cooked with fibers from Harvey Weinstein's casting couch.

Erma, my siblings and I considered SPAM and Steak-Ums delicacies. Finding the sole cherry in a tin of fruit cocktail was the ultimate jackpot. When Mom said she was making "ends meet," we thought it was the name of her actual recipe. She oftentimes left spaghetti noodles in the pot on the stove and re-boiled them in the same starchy swamp water the next night. "You will eat it, and you will like it!" she said. And we did. (As you may have guessed, she loved your quote: "Why take pride in cooking when they don't take pride in eating?")

Today, people are even spared from the back-breaking, soul-crushing, time-consuming task of grocery shopping. Instead of unloading recycled bags from one's own car trunk, corporate minions earning minimum wage push the tangible cart. One company specializes in sending rejected goods and deformed produce to the customer's doorstep. Their commercial features a carrot sprouting a tentacle being twerked by a square cantaloupe with Miley Cyrus's likeness. (Scrolling at the bottom of the screen was the message: **WARNING! THE FOLLOWING ADVERTISEMENT CONTAINS SEXUAL CONTENT AND GRAPHIC IMAGES.**)

Sometimes I think about what mealtime will look like at nursing homes in the future. There is no way folks will be catered to in the manner to which they've become accustomed. If anything, their health may dictate an altogether different special diet—clear liquids, puréed solids, and tube feedings. I can just hear the aides echoing my mom: "You will eat it, and you will like it!"

Yours truly,

Me

GET YOUR EMOTIONAL-SUPPORT DUCKS IN A ROW

Dear Erma,

I thought I had heard it all, but today's newspaper headline proved me wrong. An athlete completed the New York City marathon alongside her emotional-support Pekin duck, Wrinkle. Although its wings were presumably in perfect working order, Wrinkle waddled to the finish line in custom-made webbed sneakers. (I found it unnecessary to write "custom made," as if Eastbay keeps such items in stock.) The Aflac duck sent the duo a congratulatory DM and a form for supplemental health insurance, free for the next 26 miles.

George was obsessed with his stuffed animals as a tot: Yolk the Chicken, Porkchop the Pig, Slider the Cow, and Gyro the Lamb. (Like you once wrote, "I didn't fight my way to the top of the food chain to be a vegetarian.") I think you'll agree that such an attachment is perfectly normal, harmless, and even healthy. But now some people have chosen to deal with their psychological needs with actual living, breathing, emotional-support animals.

I'm not referring to legitimate, trained service animals that support the blind or detect oncoming seizures in epileptic patients. Nor do I mean K9s that assist law enforcement. I am talking about the bogus labels entitled wackos give their pets so laws and rules magically don't apply to them.

Trust me, Erma, they are taken *everywhere*. Dot and I were trying to enjoy lunch at our favorite bistro when a pomsky vigorously licked his butthole just steps from the beverage station. If you think that is odious, imagine my disgust finding my dental hygienist's Yorkie-poo napping in a Barkalounger next to the examination chair during my cleaning. It's no longer, "How much is that doggie in the window?" but, "What imbecile is allowing that curious puggle at the National Wildlife Refuge to dig in the nest of the endangered leatherback sea turtles?"

And if you suffer allergies like I do, well, too bad. During a recent flight, a passenger brought along her emotional-support cat, which required me to pop an emotional-support Benadryl and use four boxes of emotional-support Kleenexes. Several years ago, when returning from overseas, a security screener reprimanded me for the nectarine forgotten in my purse. Now the same suitcase could legally house a narwhal.

Remember how in the nursery rhyme *Mary Had a Little Lamb,* the fluffball was banned from the playground? If written today, the teacher would need union representation while the school district faced a seven-figure discrimination lawsuit. And, of course, the children would not be allowed to "laugh and play," as this might offend the fluffball's owner.

I've noticed that people tend to choose critters to compensate for their own perceived flaws. Hank's unmotivated coworker, for instance, has a sloth. My hairy brother-in-law just posted an ad on Craigslist seeking an abominable snowman. When my Great Aunt Maude's insurance declined her nose job, she went through some shady channels to get her hands on a Proboscis monkey from Borneo. (How abhorrent! As you once wrote, "Poached eggs are good, poached animals are not.")

I admit, at my first glimpse of back fat, I was tempted to rescue a Shar Pei. And as my jawline lost definition and my face and neck unconsciously coupled, I begged Hank to fetch me a llama. He reminded me that we had yet to dispose of Speedy's remains.

People used to rely on objects to fulfill their psychological needs. Everything worked out just fine.

As for me, I will continue to lean on my emotional-support Keurig. Bonus—it doesn't require I clean up its mess with a plastic bag.

Yours truly,

Me

PLACENTA SMOOTHIE, ANYONE?

Dear Erma,

Benjamin Franklin once said, "Nothing is certain except death, taxes, and the Duggar family overpopulating the world." To me, having nineteen kids (and counting!) is the definition of clinical insanity. Apparently, they didn't follow your advice: "Never have more children than you have car windows."

While on the subject, though, I must respectfully disagree with you on something. You wrote, "Pregnancy is the only time in a woman's life she can help God work a miracle," but if that were true, how can you explain Nancy Johnson's 1843 ice cream maker invention? She created a life-changing machine, didn't have to share credit with a man, and failed to gain an ounce.

Hank and I felt that having one offspring sounded manageable, provided he wasn't a little asshole. Or a big asshole. And don't get me started on medium-sized assholes—they're the worst; they always think they're little assholes but are always the big ones. Still, when I learned I was carrying a miracle of my own, I was positively terrified. Did the thousands of dandelion heads I snapped off while singing, "Mama had a baby and its head popped off" foreshadow poor parenting skills? Was I destined to produce a body with no brain, like the hawk tuah girl?

Hank and I did everything in our power to prepare for parenthood, including purchasing the book *Best Modern Dog Names*, and enrolling in a labor and delivery class at the local hospital. We expected an exhausting day practicing breathing exercises and pain-management techniques. Instead, a concierge gave us a tour of the newly renovated luxury birthing suites. He welcomed us "guests" (not patients, but *guests,* as if vacationing at the Magic Kingdom) with flutes of nonalcoholic Dom Pérignon and a 5-ring birth-plan binder.

The standard package at Indulgent Passages included a 1,000-square-foot space with Italian linens, marble floors, a birthing pool, peppermint-fragranced wallpaper, and furniture designed by Nate Berkus. A hypnotist, aromatherapist, massage therapist, and acupuncturist were only a text away. A Cirque du Soleil contortionist taught a positioning class to naturally accelerate labor, and Dr. Ruth Westheimer's apprentice gave tutorials on how to achieve orgasm during delivery. When Hank saw that a food ambassador, a Michelin-starred chef, would prepare a smoothie from my placenta, *his* eyes dilated ten centimeters. Placenta, we learned, contains many key nutrients. "So do bananas," he said.

Each peanut would have a portrait session with a photographer from Annie Leibovitz's internship program. All new parents would depart with a gift basket containing Oprah's Favorite Things. For a $100K upgrade, the Hollywood Star package guaranteed future admission to the college of choice and a signed 8 x 10 glossy of Felicity

Huffman.

Erma, doesn't this strike you as excessive? When you gave birth, the only luxury was the epidural itself. Like you wrote, "I had my baby when they gave you a shot in the hip and you didn't wake up until the kid was ready to start school."

I've read news headlines about infants who arrived during hurricanes and tornadoes; in subway trains and Subway restaurants; a Porta Potty and a strip club (same stench). I thought of the three thousand babies delivered by Polish midwife Stanislawa Leszczynska during her two-year internment at Auschwitz. Even the Blessed Virgin Mary gave birth surrounded by smelly livestock in a cold, dark manger. *I mean, Jesus Christ!* My own mother studied the Lamaze method from *Painless Childbirth,* and an octogenarian delivered me at home atop a *Chicago Tribune* newspaper. I often wondered if he was a veterinarian.

I never got to experience Indulgent Passages. My water broke six weeks prematurely at Babies"R"Us, and I was strapped to an ambulance gurney Hannibal Lecter-style and taken to a sketchy hospital an hour away. There, I was served lumpy Cream of Wheat, wore a tattered gown with missing rear snaps, and listened to bullets exchanged outside my window. The highlight of my stay was the obstetrician remarking during my episiotomy how she hoped to make it home in time to watch *Sons of Anarchy*. I never got a placenta smoothie.

In the end, the only thing that mattered was looking across the room, not at Oprah's Favorite Things but *mine*: Hank holding our itsy bitsy, four-and-a-half-pound son with ten fingers, ten toes, and one attached head.

Yours truly,

Me

THE GOOD ETIQUETTE, THE BAD MANNERS, AND THE UGLY SWEATPANTS

Dear Erma,

I've been meaning to ask, have you bumped into Jacqueline Kennedy Onassis yet? If so, please tell me she was wearing a pink Chanel suit with matching kitten heels and a pillbox hat. My world will shatter if she's up there lazing around in sweatpants with *Juicy* sequined across her rear-end. Likewise, I pray Jimmy Stewart hasn't traded his wool pinstripe waistcoat and pleated slacks for low-slung jeans that play peekaboo with his boxer briefs. Since you left this world, Erma, kneecaps have developed a gravitational pull.

A semi-formal dress-code was once considered an unspoken rule in certain settings, but now anything goes. I've spotted a Snuggie and moose slipper combo at an airport; a threadbare hoodie that read SLUTS LOVE BEER GUTS on the witness stand during a Court TV trial; and a Lady Gaga meat dress replica at a funeral. (And if I am being honest, red never was the decedent's best color, and meat a poor reminder of her high blood pressure.)

My high school principal kicked me out of a Halloween dance for wearing a Madonna cone bra, but today it could be worn to teach Sunday school. Apart from *The Golden Shower Bachelor* rose ceremonies, people dress like landfills.

You once wrote, "My kid was in a school play, and I ironed only the leg of the trouser that faced the audience." Ha! No one uses irons anymore. No one wears trousers. Well, some do but only if ripped in all the right places. (I've yet to figure out if they think there are any wrong places.)

It's not only attire that has changed for the worse. Etiquette has been discarded like a soiled diaper on a freeway exit ramp. Kids no longer address adults with titles Mr./Sir/Mrs./Miss/Ms./Ma'am. Instead, they call us by our first name as if their Cracker Barrel server. I blame the McDonald's Corporation because they encouraged such informality, naming their spokes-clown "Ronald" instead of "Mr. McDonald." Slippery slope, you see.

Pardon me for asking such a personal question, but did you and Bill pass gas in front of each other? During a recent happy hour with my girlfriends, I mentioned that Hank and I do no such thing. With the way their jaws hit the floor, you'd have thought I had told them something outrageous, like Leonardo DiCaprio was dating a woman his own age, a Chicago resident died of natural causes and not gunfire, or Nick Cannon got a vasectomy. (Which he hasn't because you can tell by his pants.)

People commit this sinful act anytime, any place. I have a friend who, five days into a juice cleanse, justified letting one rip during a professional massage because she was underneath a 25-pound weighted-blanket. "And anyway, it's natural," she said.

"So is Type 2 diabetes," I argued, "but it's best kept under control." Come to think of it, so is death, but there's a time and a place.

What do you make of this, Erma? I recently attended a baby shower where the mom-to-be handed out a blank envelope to each guest and instructed us to write our mailing address on the front. I assumed it was part of some silly game and had forgotten all about it when, a while later, I opened my mailbox to see my own handwriting staring back at me. Inside was a basic card printed on standard stock paper: "Thank you for showering us with love." There was no mention of the forty-eight-inch-tall diaper tower I constructed, or the U-Haul I piloted to deliver all the gifts back to her Airbnb. The card wasn't even signed! (Nor was there any information about the nameless infant, who by now had to be old enough to have filled the diaper tower several times and wear a cone bra to daycare.)

I have a favor to ask. In addition to Jackie O., could you please locate Emily Post and send her back to Earth? First-class postage and express delivery. There's a lot of work to be done. Thank you!

Yours truly, Me

OK, FREE-RANGE CHILDREN: ON YOUR MARK, GET SET, GO HOME!

Dear Erma,

The problem with my *Welcome!* mat is that my state's literacy rate is 94%. Some mornings, before the first of four hours of the *Today* show has even begun, hordes of free-range children make a pilgrimage to my house, the unofficial "it" place to be in the neighborhood. They appear out of nowhere as aliens, migraines, natural disasters, and Satan are sometimes known to do. One day the line stretched so long Google Earth mistook them for the Great Wall of China.

Upon arrival, they bang on my front door as if conducting a DEA drug bust. I attempt to hide, but the advanced youth of today have eyeballs equipped with military-grade radar capable of penetrating solid objects. You have no idea how I seethe when they breeze past the SHOES OFF, PLEASE placard in their sandy Crocs/muddy cowboy boots/sweaty Converse high-tops/sparkly *Hello Kitty!* slip-ons. They always have the same response: "Oops, my bad." (When you have a spare moment would you please tell God that if reincarnation exists, I kindly request that He assigns me to Japan in my next life? Their footwear-removal custom aligns with my deeply held values.)

One scoundrel went straight to my refrigerator and examined its contents for two full minutes while 40-degree air freely poured into the 74-degree room. I asked what he was doing and he replied, "Bruh, my mom said to have breakfast over here. BTW, what's the plan for lunch and dinner?" Honestly, what I found most offensive was that he was under the impression his Nirvana T-shirt was the latest brand of energy drink.

I didn't have time to lament because one rascal plucked our new hamster (not one word, Erma, not one word!) from his cage and placed him … well, her ADHD caused her to forget where … and now Speedy the Second is the subject of a *Crime Junkie* podcast "missing" episode. Then, we blew a fuse due to some delinquent charging his e-scooter on the same outlet as George's e-drum set. (Again, not one word, Erma, not one word! Just say no to recorders, the gateway instrument.)

On the way to the electric panel, I busted a girl sitting criss-cross applesauce as she painted her nails on the bed frame I have been trying to assemble for a month. (Rome wasn't built in a day; neither is IKEA furniture.)

The polish color was called "Winterberry Fusion," which

was also her own name. I had recognized her from several Amber Alerts. For the first, she was found at the local Furniture Warehouse jumping on mattresses and swinging from rug displays. The second time she was discovered in a glue trap in her own basement. Legit question: Can we please bring back helicopter parenting?

Erma, you once wrote, "Kids need love the most when they're acting most unlovable," which explains the reasoning behind most states' strict regulations for obtaining conceal-and-carry permits. But seriously, I needed all of them out of my dry-shampooed hair or I'd need Saul Goodman on speed dial.

Briefly, I considered having a lemonade stand, but it was too early in the day for that. Even Savannah Guthrie was still sound asleep. Besides, the simple displays you remember have turned into a Six Flags amusement park offering deep-fried churros, cotton candy, snow-cones, corn on the cob, and foot-long hot dogs. And forget the collapsible card table on the sidewalk; today's set-ups mirror a military field hospital with generators that pipe in air-conditioning and cool jazz on Spotify. That seemed like work. A lot of work. A lot of work *for me*.

Through my megaphone, I announced local occupancy ordinances and zoning codes required them to move outdoors. Well, talk about pushback! "What will we do out there? How will we survive in the wild?" they cried, *literally cried*. Given their reactions you would have assumed I was the poor woodcutter sending Hansel and Gretel deep into the forest with nothing more than a pocket of stale breadcrumbs, when in reality it was a five-hundred-pack of sugar-free blue raspberry freezies.

I took one of their smartwatches, pinned our backyard, pressed "proceed to the route," and sent the interlopers on their way. Then I deadbolted the door and changed the garage code. But forty-five seconds, Erma—forty-five seconds!—is all it took before hearing the phrase I hate more than any other in the English language: "We're bored!"

I suggested they sing *99 Bottles of Beer on the Wall,* but they felt it was age inappropriate. I urged them to hunt for four-leaf clovers, but they reasoned they could just buy them on Amazon. I chanted *George George Bo Borje Banana Fanna Foe Forge Me My Mo Morje, George,* but they pitied my sudden stuttering problem. I pleaded with them to bounce on the new trampoline, but they claimed it was too dangerous. (I pointed out that egg cartons routinely travel from an Idaho chicken coop and arrive perfectly intact to the 60th-floor of a Boston condominium, but one twerp was hyper-focused on whether the eggs originated from an organic, cage-free, free-range, or enriched-colony farm.) Espeyeff claimed she was allergic to the sun, but I assured her it would not be a problem as it hadn't even risen yet. Bobbing for apples? Not without their waterproof disposable facemasks.

My siblings and I played dodgeball with our dad's tools;

caught fireflies in jars on summer nights; did gravestone rubbings at cemeteries; played rock-paper-scissors until we developed tennis elbow; cleaned out an abandoned barn to make a roller rink; and wrote fan mail to Bill from Capitol Hill (*Schoolhouse Rock,* not Clinton). The only time we relied on adults to keep us entertained was when we trailed customers in the grocery store and waited for them to discover the Chiquita banana sticker we had stuck on the back of their shirts. (Our snickering gave it away.) We lived outside! At dusk, Mom oftentimes had no choice but to escort us back home by our earlobes.

With that in mind, I refused to let the free-rangers win. The United States doesn't negotiate with terrorists, so why should I? Instead, I took a moment to enjoy a cup of coffee and muse about how their mothers claim to prefer entertaining in their own houses. They say, "That way I know exactly where they are, who they are with, and what they are doing." *TOTAL LIARS!*

My thoughts were interrupted by pounding at the patio door. I unlocked it and a squirt darted to the bathroom holding the seat of his pants. After thirty minutes of the fan running at high speed, he came out, leaned in close to me, and enunciated like a *Wheel of Fortune* contestant when solving the puzzle, "The. Toilet. Is. Clogged." As you once wrote, Erma, "With boys, you always know where you stand. Right in the path of a hurricane."

I will write more later. I am going to the store for a plunger, and more importantly, a new front doormat. After that, I have to pick up freezie tubes scattered across my yard. I hadn't realized they were *not* sugar-free. Ooops, my bad!

Yours truly,

Me

IF CLEANLINESS IS CLOSE TO GODLINESS, I AM GOING TO HELL

Dear Erma,

George keeps his clothes on the floor of his room or in the lost-and-found box from wherever he just came. The piles *next to* his laundry basket have become so tall that a location scout inquired if his room could be their mountain climbing training facility. It was already the inspiration behind TLC network's new spinoff series, *Say Yes to the Mess.*

The disarray has gotten to the point that his coat hangers filed an unemployment claim, and the furnace filter reported us to OSHA for hazardous working conditions. The toxic fumes were akin to the olfactory assault of death that soldiers experience during war and later discuss in PTSD support groups. Before he went missing, Speedy the Second tied a noose out of his hammock and threatened to unalive himself. In all fairness, I can understand how staring at such an unpleasant landscape day after day would result in such desperation. (I "talked" him out of it because I had no more room in my freezer.)

I took Department of Homeland Security's motto, "See something, smell something, say something," seriously and reported the offending odor, hoping it could be a chemical warfare agent instead of my very own homegrown domestic terrorist. They requested oxygen and cootie samples, but unlike the Pony Express, the post office refused to handle liquid, hazardous, or perishable material. How could a sweet little boy who not long ago smelled like Nilla wafers grow up to emit a stench rivaling Vieux Boulogne cheese? (Moisture-wicking socks are a complete scam!)

I forced George to listen to an old vinyl of "The Gambler," but Kenny Rogers' wisdom about knowing what to keep and what to toss flew over his head. The sole remaining strategy I had up my rolled-up sleeves was to use *Spark Joy* by Marie Kondo as a life raft in our domestic apocalypse.

Erma, you once warned, "Housework, if it is done properly, can cause brain damage," so prior to reading the first page, I scheduled an appointment with a neurologist. And because you also wrote, "Cleaning the house while the children are home is like shoveling while it's still snowing," I shipped Hank and George off on a father/son geocaching excursion in Iceland. Two-week deluxe package with a three-day layover in Reykjavik. Nothing but the best for my little mess-makers.

Ms. Kondo insists that mental clarity comes from decluttering, clearly unaware of the IRS's recommendation to retain tax documents for seven years. She also suggests adding a small ornamental plant, but with my luck it would veg out all day watching *The Real Houseplants of Greenhouse.* And her vision of a serene, refreshing bathroom? Let's just say she hasn't met a boy who pops fiber gummies as if Tic Tacs.

The kitchen was the most challenging room to tackle because

the island is like Bora Bora, the ultimate vacation destination where the contents of my entire house yearn to travel. Refrigerator magnets that read, PLEASE EXCUSE THE MESS. OUR CHILDREN ARE MAKING MEMORIES, and GOOD MOMS HAVE STICKY FLOORS, MESSY KITCHENS, DIRTY OVENS, LAUNDRY PILES, AND HAPPY CHILDREN, should be considered nothing more than dangerous propaganda marketed by the *Hoarders* filming crew.

I felt it was professionally negligent for her to omit the subject of glitter. You never mentioned it in your newspaper column, "Operation Dustrag," either. There really should be more public awareness campaigns about the dangers of this arts-n-crafts squatter that gets everywhere even when the jar is not open. How so many people are obsessed with anything so evil is beyond me, but I suppose even serial killers have fan clubs.

On a positive note, I finally learned how to properly fold a shirt, the reason cited on my 1991 termination slip from GAP. Also, I am now able to remove fingerprints, fibers, blood, DNA, and fecal matter with the efficiency of a professional hitman, and one never knows when that skill can come in handy.

Still, I just wish life could be like in *The Elves and the Shoemaker*, but instead of waking up each morning to find bespoke footwear, I'd have a mudroom that did not live up to its name. (George's soccer cleats gift the floor with so many grass clippings it could pass for Astroturf.)

If nothing else, I am hopeful that I will begin to claim a higher annual income than the couch cushions. (So far this year they have collected $6.22 combined.) A news article reporting stay-at-home-moms should be earning $178,201 has made me reexamine my life.

The house in which I grew up didn't even have a vacuum cleaner—only a broom, dustpan, and carpet sweeper. My mom's organizational system didn't entail stacks of matching bins with cute mini chalkboard labels. She used a large bag containing medium bags containing small bags containing tiny bags. It was like a plastic bag version of matryoshka dolls. Her antibacterial spray? Her own spit.

Sadly, I found the remains of Speedy the Second in the vacuum's lint canister. (They were the exact gray color of house #1392.) Ugh, some things are best left swept under the rug.

Yours truly,

Me

COLOR ME HAPPY, BARISTA!

Dear Erma,

This morning, I entered Starbucks and received my drink an hour and a half later. I have attended Palm Sunday mass when the priest read the entire Passion of Jesus and baptized septuplets in less time.

The customer ahead of me cleared her throat, took a deep breath, then spouted her order: an organic, extra hot, red-eye latte with pi amount of soy and the remaining amount in coconut milk, half-pump peppermint syrup, 1/32 teaspoon of chestnut powder, lite caramel drizzle, no foam, fat-free whip with equal pumps of Tahitian vanilla, Mexican vanilla, Madagascar vanilla, French vanilla, pure vanilla extract, and sugar-free vanilla sprinkles. It took longer for her to recite than "The Wreck of the Edmund Fitzgerald" played in its entirety. Was there even room for the java after all that junk?

The barista acted as if such rigmarole was completely standard. He didn't even flinch. Instead, he typed the order into the register faster than a court reporter transcribing the Johnny Depp v. Amber Heard trial. (And I can barely punch in my home security code on the keypad before a squad car is dispatched to my residence.) He took a bow when he presented the beverage to the customer.

When it was my turn, I asked for a black coffee. His acerbic glare reminded me of Putin, so I requested a plain hot tea instead and he threatened to call a priest to have me exorcised.

You once wrote, "The odds of going to the store for a loaf of bread and coming out with only a loaf of bread are three billion to one." The same could be said about going to a café today and ordering a beverage with fewer than three syllables. I left with a plastic water bottle that Putin said would take 450 years to decompose.

On my way out, I passed a selfish individual single-handedly occupying a twelve-person conference table. Next to her was a stack of adult coloring books and a ten thousand pack of crayons, which resembled Holland's Keukenhof Tulip Gardens. Erma, Madame Tussaud's Museum didn't have the amount of wax as the kaleidoscopic sea in front of her. A grown woman, old enough to have used actual toxic crayons when they were legal, has been replaced by an inner child. *Was I the subject of a TikTok prank?*

I decided to drop in to check on Great Aunt Maude. Her health rapidly declined after contracting herpes at The Villages retirement community, and she had no choice but to surrender her emotional-support Proboscis monkey and transfer to a nursing home. (I didn't think it was possible for her sour disposition to become more insufferable, but when there's a will there's a way.)

Normally the residents love to have visitors, but Great Aunt Maude completely ignored me and continued detailing paisley, ikat, trellis, honeycomb, and fleur-de-lis designs in her adult coloring book. After stealing her lukewarm cranberry juice cocktail, I just went home.

Back in my day, coloring books were the go-to item for any gift exchange. In early November, local supermarkets handed them out to customers and sponsored contests for the brightest, most festive-looking turkey. Library story hour began with coloring time. Pediatrician offices plastered their patients' creations all over the walls.

Now the only place left to find a printed sheet is a restaurant children's menu (***only for ages ten and under). Even then, it is muddied with connect-the-dots, crossword puzzles, and word finds. Whose budget and waistline can afford to indulge whenever their budding Picasso wants to express himself? Not mine. The traditional format has become impossible to find. Today, there are better odds of Zohran Mamdani wearing a red MAGA hat than locating a child's coloring book on the shelf of Dollar Tree, Family Dollar, or Dollar General.

Unfortunately, little ones are unable to use the more advanced adult coloring books because their brain activity has flatlined from thousands of hours staring at screens. Complex illustrations would prove far too overwhelming, so they need simple 2D images of sailboats, bananas, farmers holding rakes, Saturn, kittens batting a ball of yarn, and fairies waving at a happy fish. In the future, if such coloring books are in mint condition, they will fetch as much money as the December, 1953 *Playboy* issue featuring a centerfold of Marilyn Monroe.

Grown-ups have also completely overtaken other activities traditionally ***only for ages ten and under: kickball, frisbee, dodgeball, jump rope, and yo-yo leagues with official uniforms and paid referees. I will never become accustomed to seeing someone old enough to have used the expression, "Go fly a kite," *actually* flying a kite. Who do they think they are reverting to infancy like that, Benjamin Button?

Tomorrow, I plan to enjoy my black coffee at home. And when I ponder why life had to change at all, the only thing I will draw is a blank.

Yours truly,

Me

BEAUTY IS IN THE EYE OF THE CREDIT CARD HOLDER

Dear Erma,

When someone asks, "With that price, how can you go wrong?" it can be entertaining to stick around to see what happens next. Unless you are a vain eight-year-old girl whose mother added a fifth cardinal virtue to include frugality and she has just learned the local beauty school charges fifty cents for a haircut, in which case, RUN!

The training academy was on the third level of a decrepit building overlooking the county jail. After Mom prepaid for services and signed an arbitration agreement, we took our seats next to a wall of plastic mannequin heads with patchy tufts of hair, half-melted ears, and drips of eggplant-colored dye stained onto their cheeks. They looked like burn victims who never learned to stop, drop, and roll during fire safety week. You once wrote, "Never go to a doctor whose office plants have died." You should have added, "and a beauty salon displaying props from *The Walking Dead.*" I left looking more like Mark Hamill than Dorothy Hamill. And my brother? We told everyone he had male pattern baldness—at age five.

After that, my grandpa cut my hair for free. Since I was up to date on my vaccinations, Mom wasn't concerned that he used the same pair of rusty scissors to cut fat off a slab of New York strip or skin off a trout. Grandpa later explained that cutting hair was a lot like writing on a chalkboard. Up close, he was certain he was forming a straight line, but after taking a step back he realized, *Whoa.* Attempting to correct it only made the *other side* uneven, so he continued snipping, left to right, right to left, shorter and shorter, my bangs playing teeter-totter across my forehead until I looked like a juvenile Mark Zuckerberg. (The Bible should have included my before and after photos next to Job 1:21: "The Lord giveth and the Lord taketh away.") Like I said, Mom was frugal, and we didn't have to tip Grandpa.

You once wrote, "If I raised my hand to wipe the hair out of my children's eyes, they'd flinch and call their attorney." I get it. The next time Mom called Grandpa, I contacted an attorney specializing in the emancipation of minors. I vowed that if I ever had a kiddo of my own, I would take him to a real salon, not an institution for higher learning or the home of a retired relative with cataracts, claw hand syndrome, and an Afghan hound named Pixie.

True to my word, when a sports-themed barbershop opened in our neighborhood, I knew it would be the perfect place to take George. Little did I know that we'd be entering Wrigley Field. Flat-screen televisions the size of fire-station garage doors hung on every wall broadcasting live Major League Baseball games. We walked past the security guard, checked in with the ticket sales agent, and took our seats on the bleachers. Erma, you remember just how uncomfortable they were! Was I ever relieved when I was handed a stadium seat cushion with the company's logo. A vendor came through hollering, "Peanuts, get your fresh roasted peanuts!" and they smelled scrumptious!

Soon, a stylist dressed as an umpire announced that George was up to bat. She tied a cape around his neck with "MVP" embroidered in metallic threads and asked, "How can I make your day a home run?"

I am not sure how much time passed (the pipe organist playing "Charge!" must have put me in some kind of trance), but when I looked up, George was missing! I catapulted across the salon—ducking to miss a promotional T-shirt shot from an air cannon—and sprinted to the "locker room." There he was, reclining in a leather spa chair, his face shrouded in steaming white towels and lower legs encased in paraffin wax. (I admit it, Erma, I was jealous. Eight pedicurists, three podiatrists, and countless shoe salespeople working 100% on commission have refused to come anywhere near my feet.)

I collected George and went to pay the bill. On my "scoreboard" was an itemized list of expenses incurred for my little "all-star:" Shears Transformation: $75. Stadium Seat Pad: $30. Concessions: $20. Grand-Slam Locker-Room Treatment: $70. The total was $195, not including tax and tip. A ticket to the World Series wouldn't have cost as much.

I reflected upon my haircuts at the beauty school and Grandpa's. And I imagined my mother, whom I endlessly ridiculed for her thrifty ways, saying, "With that price, how can you go wrong?"

Once again, she was right. Mothers are *always* right. But you knew that already.

Yours truly,

Me

SIRI, WHAT'S AN ENCYCLOPEDIA?

Dear Erma,

I am on a roll! Once again, I proved I'm not a robot (and I didn't even have to get off the couch)! Granted, it took four attempts to correctly mark the crosswalks, palm trees, traffic lights, and motorcycles, but the hassle proved worthwhile when I received the following confirmation: "Great news! You are officially human!" (The last congratulatory message I received was from eBay informing me I won the auction for a pre-owned CorningWare gravy boat in acceptable condition.)

But as I basked in the glory, my biggest fear came to fruition. George asked to get his own phone. I felt the panic one might experience witnessing someone twitch in his sleep, hoping he was having a dream and not a grand mal seizure.

As his parent, I feel responsible for providing a tool to develop and strengthen his friendships through meaningful conversations. But he certainly did not need a device capable of alien communication, mind reading, and time travel. Additionally, studies have shown that they are addictive, and human DNA structures are evolving to the point that babies are born with hands resembling Lego characters and eyes like nocturnal marsupials.

After much consideration I offered to install a landline, which he likened to carving hieroglyphics into cave walls with dinosaur bone. "All you can do on those is *talk*," he protested.

When I was in high school my mom implemented a strict fifteen-minute-per-day limit on our bile-colored rotary dial phone, which was attached to the wall next to the bile-colored refrigerator. Three of those minutes were spent fingering the rotary dial because too many friends had a 9 in their phone number. "Can you hear me now?" wasn't a catchy marketing phrase but a fair question after the fatigued coil stretched clear across the kitchen, down the hallway, into the living room, and around the corner into the broom closet. My little brothers often used it as a limbo bar.

I'm sure you remember the dreaded *beep beep beep* of a busy signal, which happened if either the line was already in use or the receiver wasn't hung up correctly. (There was such satisfaction in slamming it down, wasn't there? Doing so now results in a shattered screen and an emergency trip to the mini mall, beginning a conversation with an 11-year-old Apple genius and a new contract with thirty-six monthly installation payments.)

It's unheard of now, but my family used to share a party line with two other families. Contrary to its name, party lines were no cause for celebration and had nothing to do with cocaine (unless my Great Aunt Maude's fifth husband was "on the line"). However, my tightwad father considered the $1.30 shaved off our monthly bill worth intrusive neighbors spying on our calls. When I described this arrangement to George, his eyes got as big as PopSockets.

"Don't confuse fame with success. Fame is Madonna; Helen Keller is the other," was such an astute observation of yours and rings true now more than ever. Social media influencers (A.K.A. former reality television contestants or nepo babies) do not understand this key difference. To them, attention is attention.

It sickens me that George wants to waste his time following these narcissists and watching irrelevant ads from their sponsors. How I miss the days when "followers" were the twelve disciples who stalked Jesus, housewives who never missed an episode of *All My Children,* or those who trailed Forrest Gump on his impromptu run across America. "Sponsors" pertained to Alcoholics Anonymous and the volunteers promising Christian youth guidance during confirmation.

Furthermore, I never thought I'd live in an era when going viral is the goal. It's as if no one gives the proper reverence to meningitis or Ebola anymore.

What if George stumbled upon porn when doomscrolling? He would be shocked to discover anything racier than hot felon mugshots or a Super Bowl wardrobe malfunction. Even stumbling upon his babysitter's Instagram would be confusing. In her profile picture she is wearing a skimpy tank top that reads:

when the only sandwich she ever made for him was a lousy peanut butter and jelly.

It used to take effort to find X-rated images, like subscribing to a television channel or visiting an adult bookstore. My dad, for instance, was too cheap to even buy a magazine. He would just watch the *Solid Gold* dancers then retire early for the night.

Even though George hates taking quizzes at school, I can see him willingly providing the name of his first pet along with the last thing he ate to find out what his stripper's name is. Speedy/Molasses shouldn't be cheapened like that. Or Pop-Tarts, for that matter. Though, in fairness, Speedy Tart is a good stripper name. Molasses Pop is not.

I also have concerns that George would misuse it doing his homework. The wise, mature, classy wife you and I knew as *Encyclopedia Britannica* has been replaced with a lenient, enabling, know-it-all mistress named Siri. And even *she* was dumped (they always are) in favor of mysterious artificial intelligence. AI won't insist he grab a dictionary to learn the proper spelling of M I S S I S S I P P I or make him memorize his multiplication tables. Basically, it's a willing accomplice to cheating, the technological version of Lori Laughlin and Mossimo Giannulli.

Much to my dismay, texting is frequently used in place of face-to-face communication. My mom announced dinner was ready by standing on the front porch and beating a potato masher on a mixing bowl. I can see George texting me to bring him and his friends some saltines covered in lard when we are in the same room. Of course, it wouldn't take long to learn that group chats are impossible to leave. Katie Holmes may be the only person capable of pulling it off.

I just don't want George's impressionable mind cluttered with meaningless rubbish. Spam and robocalls would bombard him with opportunities to improve his credit score. *A credit score for someone who gets $5 a week allowance!* Additionally, anyone who would brag about getting Wordle on the second try is too full of himself (and too smart) to associate with us. Surely, he would realize it was a bad idea the first time a friend hijacked his weekend with a docuseries-length photo dump of his vacation. Patience is not his best trait, and one can tolerate seeing only so many pictures of another's feet buried in the sand along with the caption, "Living my best life!"

It is frightening how algorithms know every detail about a person. For example, Facebook has suggested I join the group "Recipes for Meat-n-Potato Types" and is running repeated Lipitor ads.

Don't get me started on the endless social media challenges. George laughs when I challenge him to clean his room. When I was his age, it was common knowledge that the Jerry Lewis telethon was about raising money and awareness for muscular dystrophy, but participants today have no clue why they are dumping buckets of ice water over their stupid heads. Worse yet are the outrageous, dangerous stunts such as car surfing, eating spoonfuls of cinnamon, or shoving innumerable marshmallows into their mouths.

Erma, I cannot tell you how much I abhor being nominated to post inspirational pictures for ten days in a row. "No words, no explanation, GO!" *Ten days*, Erma! That's how long it takes to find a parking spot at Trader Joe's. When someone posts a trail of hearts along with the word "THIS!" or "Happy heavenly birthday, Grandma," I know, without even reading it, to grab a handkerchief.

In the event he did use the phone for conversational purposes, he would use Bluetooth earbuds, leaving people to assume he forgot to remove his Q-tips.

Okay, it's settled. George is not getting a phone yet. Sure, he might be angry, but once he simmers down, he'll realize that I never make him prove he's not a robot. *That* is true love.

If he needs to reach Hank or me in event of an emergency, surely, he can find a quarter. A pay phone, though … hmmm, that might be a problem.

Yours truly,

Me

LIGHTS, CAMERA, FILTERS, ACTION!

Dear Erma,

When the Department of Motor Vehicles answers customer phone calls by saying, "It's a great day! I'd be more than happy to help you!" I can understand why some mistrust our government.

It was time for me to get an enhanced driver's license, which meant being humiliated in person instead of staying dignified online. The parking lot was full, and I circled around so many times my Kia identified as a Spirograph. I found a spot sandwiched between an electric vehicle-charging station and a double-parked sedan with a bumper sticker that read: MY BMW IS SMARTER THAN YOUR HONOR STUDENT.

The line into the building extended out the door, around the block, and down the sidewalk. After verifying it wasn't a Black Friday sale, the Chick-fil-A drive-thru, or a reenactment of the 2024 election polls, I ripped a number tab off the paper roll, like at the deli. Then I took my place in line behind a woman binging *Grey's Anatomy* on her phone. Only sixteen more seasons to go.

I should add that it was ninety-three degrees out, which wasn't the ideal time to try natural deodorant. I hadn't been so saturated since I sat in the front row at a Gallagher show and he whacked an organic watermelon with a participation trophy. The worst part was having to hold my pee, although I *did* reach my daily goal of ten thousand steps marching in place.

Midway through *Grey's Anatomy* season 5, I finally made it into the building only to learn the air-conditioning was out and every seat was occupied by dudes manspreading the wingspan of the wandering albatross.

At last, the clerk called my number. But although industrial-sized, oscillating fans blew in every direction, the internal temperature soared to that of a hot rod's engine block. Heatstroke had taken hold, and I was in the initial stages of delirium. Instead of asking to renew my license, I approached the counter and demanded a pound of ham and a quart of potato salad.

Unfortunately, I regained lucidity long enough to have my picture taken. Beyoncé looked glorious onstage with breeze-blown hair and dewy makeup, but I wasn't as blessed. I wasn't a *hot* mess, just a *regular* mess, and my photo looked like an advertisement for a decongestant commercial. "Enhanced," it turned out, meant *extra* ugly. (Wouldn't you agree that it's only fair that state employees, like physicians, be mandated to take the Hippocratic Oath to do no harm?)

I spent my evening depressed and watched a beauty vlogger provide hair and makeup tutorials and hacks. With eyelashes extensions longer than EVA foam brushes in an automated carwash, hair Rapunzel would envy, pores like cellophane, and a waistline of a wet paper straw, she looked like a cartoon character. Her device's facial recognition software must glitch out all the time.

She was promoting her master class titled, "Achieving an Artful Selfie," which covered topics such as tips on not falling off cliff edges; bathroom faux pas (i.e. failing to flush the toilet or remove drug paraphernalia prior to taking the shot); gang symbols 101; and photogenic entrées to order when pretending to eat a meal. Bonus content included millions of reasons why no male, under any circumstances, should ever ever ever send a dick pic.

Forget absolving the world of cancer or finding a solution for homelessness. Photoshop is the greatest of superpowers. Like the Dalai Lama said, "The goal is not to be better than the other man but your previous self."

If only you could see pictures of me growing up. I never looked like the darling girls on the Lifetouch school flyers. In fact, a lippy classmate nicknamed me "Clearasil Cabbage Patch Kid." (To his credit, it was an accurate comparison, making the jab sting all the greater.) In fourth grade I had an impetigo outbreak and concealed the oozing pustules by holding my teddy bear in front of my chin. Today, my mom would have simply paid the $8 retouching fee, cheaper than going to a med spa for a $275 snail-slime facial.

In our 1979 church directory, my family is positioned in front of a mountain landscape, a curious backdrop given the congregation consisted mostly of Midwestern dairy farmers. The photo shoot took place in the basement typically reserved for breastfeeding mothers and naughty children disrupting Pastor Markson's sermon laughing at breastfeeding mothers.

No effort was made to coordinate outfits, and we looked like actors on a studio backlot simultaneously shooting film scenes in different genres. My younger sister wore a Betty Boop top, a candy bracelet, and plastic earrings the size of Hula-Hoops. My little brother had on a Garanimals turtleneck with FOOTBALL☆ printed on the front, and corduroy pants that concealed corrective leg braces. (Initially considered a hindrance, the bar splints allowed the photographer, Pastor Markson's wife, to lift him like a six-pack and position him as desired). Mom forced my older sister to show off her Girl Scout uniform and beret combo. (Her vengeful eyes and scornful expression contradicted the group's mission to make the world a better place.) My lavender dress from Goodwill made me break out in a terrible rash. I begged for time to let the welts subside, but it was nearly time to pass the collection plate. (If only there was a chip-reader.)

As for my parents, Dad sported a clay-colored leisure suit, a bolo tie, and bushy sideburns that stuck out as far as an

Elizabethan collar. Mom, eight months pregnant, wore a homemade gingham maternity tunic with miniature pompoms at the hem, leftover fabric from the kitchen curtains she made on her Singer Model 457 sewing machine.

Due to airbrushing and filters, if the portrait were taken today, I wouldn't recognize my own relatives. Or myself. Instead, we would be hillbilly versions of the models in Robert Palmer's *Addicted to Love* video, pretending to play banjos instead of guitars.

I treasure the averageness, realness, and imperfectness of those old snapshots. Long after I am gone from this earth and future descendants see my horrid driver's license and other photos, do you think they will notice my coffee-stained smile, the up-do that turned into an up-don't, or the uneven haircut from Grandpa? My guess … my hope … is that my dear son will share the same sentiment you wrote of your own father's death: "I didn't know his leaving would hurt so much."

Yours truly,

Me

CALGON, TAKE ME AWAY... TO MEXICO

Dear Erma,

Whoever said that being a SAHM was the best job in the world has never been awakened at 3 a.m. to high-pitched shrieking, "Mommy, my fart landed on the floor! And it's green!"

George's bathroom looked like the stage at the Nickelodeon Kids' Choice Awards. I hadn't been speechless since discovering *The View* was still on the air. I collapsed to my knees, not to clean, but to pray like Jenny from *Forrest Gump*. "Dear God, make me a bird so I can fly far, far away from here."

And of course, you remember when the boy who binged blue raspberry freezies clogged my toilet not too long ago. Well, it has never quite recovered. Nor have I. I can survive many things—a global pandemic, forever chemicals in my tap water, and Charlie Hunnam's uncanny portrayal of Ed Gein. But I cannot handle a chronically clogged toilet, and I was left with little choice but to hire an organic sewage interventionist at $325 per hour. He reminded me of a former boyfriend from decades ago who always carried around a plastic fork in his pocket in event of an emergency mash. Of course, at the time I mocked him mercilessly, but after much introspection I have come to appreciate his preparedness, problem-solving ability, and considerate nature. I heard he invented Poo-Pourri.

Hank sensed I was a flight risk and surprised me with a weekend getaway to a "mom retreat" in Cancun. The brochure featured a woman relaxing in an oversized tub with cucumbers covering her eyes. But instead of being thrilled, I ruefully thought of my poor mother, whose only escape was "Calgon, take me away" commercials. *A mom retreat.* What a load of self-indulgent nonsense! The truth was, I really didn't want to go anywhere. In fact, I preferred he and George leave for a few days, and I stay in the house alone. *If the toilet started gurgling and no one was around, would it make any sound?*

But the package included a wide range of activities, including an introduction to the Spanish language course taught by Hilaria Baldwin, so I thought, *What the heck?* When the airport shuttle dropped me off at the resort, I was greeted by a Mariachi band, which I consider to be the horrific Mexican equivalent of Christmas carolers. Whenever I see them approach, I panic. I mean, what do they want from me? Pesos, a round of Rum Chata shots, Salma Hayek returned to Coatzacoalcos? How can their only desire be to spread cheer by singing *Cielito Lindo*? In this world, not a chance.

Just between you and me, I was most excited about the

hotel. Ever since I was a young girl, I have romanticized the experience and consider it a luxurious treat. Eloise first sparked my interest (the tippy-top floor of the Plaza in New York City!). Then there was *The Shining*; spine-chilling, but at least I wouldn't have to share a room with my four siblings. Next, Julia Roberts starred in *Pretty Woman* and somehow made flossing strawberry seeds from her teeth seem mysterious and sexy.

Most of all, I looked forward to the housekeeping staff. Returning to my room to fresh coffee packets, a turned-down bed, and a stack of towels rolled up like Cinnabons seemed like a dream. Normally in hotels, I am smooshed between a diagonally sleeping ninja and the loudest snorer in the *Guinness Book of World Records*.

Despite a peaceful night's sleep, I woke up in immense pain from a pulled hamstring. (Darting away from beach vendors selling "Free Britney" serapes was not without consequence. Why can't they take a hint that their presence is unwanted? When I over-tweezed my eyebrows in the summer of 1983, they never came back; what makes these sandpreneurs so persistent?)

I figured stretching might help and sought the wellness studio. Unfortunately, I soon learned that GOAT yoga did not entail doing downward-facing dog with Serena Williams, Mia Hamm, or Simone Biles. Instead, clients received a chiropractic adjustment from a stinky, twitchy animal who enjoyed eating garbage (the one exception being Brooklyn Beckham's cooking). I looked for a spot of grass to set my mat, but piles of dung were littered everywhere. Using my foam brick to battle swarming flies disrupted the zen, and I got expelled from the class.

I retreated to a poolside lounge chair and enjoyed ~~uno dos tres~~ quatro margaritas the size of koi ponds. After my siesta, I stumbled back to my suite and saw my reflection in the bathroom mirror. My sunburn was as red as Tapatio hot sauce! I suddenly understood why the geographical location was called the Tropic of Skin Cancer. You once wrote, "When you look like your passport photo, it's time to go home," but I looked like Elmo's passport photo. I spent the rest of the weekend spread out on the bed like the Vitruvian Man, only moving to apply aloe vera.

Before catching my airport shuttle, I asked the housekeeper, Paloma G., (who according to her nametag, proudly served this establishment since 2015,) if she would consider going home with me. She responded by handing me an empty gratuity envelope and saying, "Adios by nueve o'clock."

On the long flight home, I fantasized about my family rushing to embrace me at baggage claim. But I got nada. It was the same when my Uber driver dropped me off at home. "Hello? Hello???" I called out but no one was there.

Instead of being angry, I thought, *Yes, finally, some alone time! Exactly what I wanted all along. Perfecto!*

Yours truly, Me

TRAUMA DRAMA MAMA

Dear Erma,

It's 1:33 a.m. and Hank's snoring is keeping me wide awake. Our bedroom sounds as if a grizzly bear is hibernating in a cozy shiplapped den decorated by Joanna Gaines. The old wives' tale suggests counting sheep, but what about stab wounds?

Why do you suppose traditional wedding vows make no mention of this dreadful bodily function? I promised to persevere through abject poverty and debilitating illness, but I never signed up for sleep apnea. When I mutter obscenities with every toss and turn, Siri automatically provides a list of teletherapists with immediate availability.

Therapy therapy therapy! The world insists it's the cure for any problem. Podcasts are interrupted with commercials urging listeners to discover their authentic selves with a behavior analyst. Magazines are packed with advertisements encouraging readers to use their voice and speak their truth with a licensed counselor. Public restroom stalls are surrounded by hotline numbers with volunteers waiting to lend a compassionate ear. Erma, it's to the point I can't even eat a pint of Ben and Jerry's right out of the tub in the supermarket anymore without management insisting I seek professional help.

I fully acknowledge that it can be a useful tool, but don't you find it excessive, patronizing, and even dangerous to suggest every single minor annoyance requires a psychologist? The word "trauma" should be reserved for things like watching Prince Harry's documentary or having the misfortune of having the name "Karen" or "Brandon."

Dumpster fires are a normal part of life. Always have been, always will be. Why should I consult a stranger who would only tell me to squeeze a latex-free stress ball and rake a desktop sandbox? In my experience, the best medicine is wearing dirty sweatpants and drinking dirty martinis with dirty-mouthed friends. If I can survive Great Aunt Maude, I can survive anything.

Don't even get me started on the cost. Charlie Brown got a steal when Lucy charged only a nickel for advice. (I remember my mom saying, "With that price, how can you go wrong?")

Congratulations for being married to Bill for forty-six-plus years. How impressive! Hank, aside from his snoring, is a wonderful husband too. If our marriage was a movie, I would rate him 96% on Rotten Tomatoes' Tomatometer. But like you wrote, "God created man, but I could do better," and to be perfectly honest, there are a handful of tweaks I'd make. Since I don't feel that my frustrations merit a mental health evaluation, I'm going to share them with you instead.

1. Is the "man cold" a 21st century affliction or did Bill also plead for chicken soup with stars when he had the sniffles? The way Hank dabs tissues on his runny nose reminds me of the way Bob Ross painted an evergreen tree on canvas. His long, pitiful sighs make him sound like a yodeler with a tracheostomy. Such nonsense has turned my bedside manner from Florence Nightingale into Dexter.

2. He leaves his socks as singles instead of rolling them into pairs. His dresser drawer looks like Tinder.

3. He uses the same bar of soap to wash his face as the rest of his body.

4. He mysteriously stayed sound asleep during George's shart-on-the-floor incident.

5. He keeps medication decades past its expiration date, denying the active ingredients in his snake oil lost effectiveness in the Reagan administration.

6. He refuses to use a CPAP machine, which would prevent snoring.

This might be too much information, but like many other couples, we occasionally squabble about sex. I blame the weather. You remember how cold Midwestern winters can be. Foreplay lasts only two-and-a-half minutes, precisely the time it takes to preheat the mattress pad. To us, rough sex means taking an elbow to the ribs while removing our flannel pajamas and then, since heat rises, arguing over who gets to be on top.

As you once wrote, "Marriage has no guarantees. If that's what you're looking for, go live with a car battery." But a car battery can't reassure me I don't look fat in my mom jeans (which are back in style, except for actual moms like me).

Several years ago, I went through major depression. My hygiene and beauty regime had become spotty; my toothbrush and cosmetic bag were seen stomping down the street arm-in-arm discussing abandonment issues. My hair was overdue for color and mousey roots stood up vertically along my part as if giving the middle finger. With a thirty-pound weight gain, I looked like Humpty Dumpty after he fell off the wall—round, cracked, and unsalvageable. But whenever I joked about our resemblance, Hank vehemently objected and gushed how beautiful I was. His unconditional love and acceptance helped me ineffably.

Life is full of struggles, we just have to persevere the best way we can. In sickness and in health, for richer or poorer, better and for worse, in good times and in bad, til death do us shart.

Yours truly,

Me

I'M NOT OLD ENOUGH TO BE VINTAGE

Dear Erma,

I'm a sucker for anything antique: skeleton keys, glass doorknobs, and cosmetics without a California Proposition 65 label warning of cancerous toxins. So, when I received a charming flyer for a vintage market showcasing a typewriter decades older than your IBM Selectric II, I could not wait!

The event was held in a field at the county fairgrounds. On my hike across the parking lot, I passed a group of queenagers drinking MOMosas, tailgating by their minivans wearing matching Uggs, ripped jeans, and buffalo plaid flannel shirts. Do you think Paul Bunyan would have chosen a different career path knowing the trees that he busted his ass lumberjacking would end up as lazy Susans with "Mama Bear" carved into the acacia?

Music blasted through the loudspeakers as I entered through the admissions gate. I expected to hear tunes reminiscent of *The Lawrence Welk Show*, but it was "Who Let the Dogs Out?" Booth after booth, Erma, the only things for sale were Kate Spade handbag knockoffs, crystals boasting magical powers, the very Amish fireplace my mother once blew an entire paycheck on, and everything ever advertised on *As Seen on TV*. Every vendor displayed a "shop local" sign—even the ones based out of Canada. I felt as if I was at a Long Island flea market instead of a Midwestern livestock barn.

I soon realized why there were ATMs distributed throughout the grounds. Fifteen dollars for a Mason jar of rhubarb jam. Thirty bucks for a pouch of artisanal granola. Fifty smackaroos for five pounds of grass-fed ground beef. My entire life, I was under the impression that farmers were poor.

My mom shopped at the Budget Bakery, a store that sold defective or expired goods at discounted prices. "It all ends up in the same place," she said. "And anyway, I didn't breastfeed you through kindergarten for your immune systems not to be prepared for this sort of thing." Never would she have spent five dollars for one peanut butter cookie, even with a cute criss-cross on the top.

I approached a young woman wearing a Rolling Stones jacket to ask if she'd seen them in concert, but as I got closer, I realized it read: POLLING STONES, a grassroots organization providing painted rocks with inspirational messages to anyone vowing to support their referendum on the November ballot. One rock cost $10 (or three for $29) with an additional $5 convenience fee, $4 service charge, $3 environmental tax, 20% mandatory gratuity, and a $1.50

miscellaneous surcharge. Customers were also guilted into rounding up for charity. This month, it was dolphins suffering from alopecia. The entire transaction was done "contactless," which had previously only pertained to car washes, prison visitation rooms, and Liza Minnelli's marriages.

When I stopped at the restroom, the line extended through the barn door and around the building. Not since Kmart Blue Light Specials and layaway lines had I seen women congregate in such numbers. Since the men's room had no line at all, I snuck in there and expected to have the place to myself. Nope. Dozens of disheveled, whimpering men huddled together like Emperor Penguins trying to survive in Antarctica. "Please, we beg of you, don't let our wives know where we are," one whispered, as if caught on Jeffrey Epstein's island.

Like you wrote, "Shopping is a woman thing. It's a contact sport like football. Women enjoy the scrimmage, the noisy crowds, the danger of being trampled to death, and the ecstasy of the purchase." Those fools should have stayed home.

What a disappointment the vintage market turned out to be. There were no skeleton keys, glass doorknobs, or mechanical typewriters. In fact, the oldest thing turned out to be me—and I'm not cheap either.

Yours truly,

Me

THE GLASS IS HALF-EMPTY, I'M POSITIVE

Dear Erma,

Apologies in advance, but I am a grouch today. Every minuscule thing annoys me: "6-7" being Dictionary.com's 2025 word of the year, porch pirates failing to leave thank you notes, and the U.S. penny retiring before Hank and I are financially able to do so.

What really got under my skin, though, was my coffee drive-thru experience. When I pulled ahead to pay, the cashier told me that the previous customer took care of it. *What?* It seemed too good to be true, like when celebrities threaten to leave the country if their candidate isn't elected. No rational person would throw away hard-earned money on a stranger and expect nothing in return.

I noticed that the car's bumper stickers read, "BE HAPPY" and "CHOOSE JOY." Yes, all caps. Erma, I am not against the philosophy, but I find the bossy tone irksome. Had the Nike corporation chosen "*Please,* Just Do It" as their slogan, I may have done a few jumping jacks.

This overt positivity movement is out of control. Just last

week it became illegal to manufacture and distribute throw pillows unless embroidered with the aforementioned phrases. The statute was swiftly amended to include: "LIVE LAUGH LOVE" and "THANKFUL GRATEFUL BLESSED." "EAT PRAY LOVE" would have been included, but there was a copyright issue. It seems, Erma, that you can be all kinds of happy hippie or positive psychobabbler, but you can't just give good vibes away.

We are not subscribers to the Optimism-on-Demand network capable of intentionally selecting our moods. Constant merriness is not realistic, and emotional nosedives should not be considered taboo. As you once wrote, "If life is a bowl of cherries, what am I doing in the pits?"

Hold on, *Magnum P.I.* is being interrupted with breaking news…

Oh, my goodness! This morning, a coffee chain 1,478 customers long was broken. What kind of jerk would do such a thing? Disgusting.

Yours truly,

Me

IT TAKES A VILLAGE TO FUNDRAISE A CHILD

Dear Erma,

Ahhh, remember the good old days when "must accept all cookies in order to function properly" was nothing more than a Girl Scout's pitch to sell boxes of Thin Mints? When I was in fifth grade, I desperately wanted to attend summer camp, an experience my parents felt I would appreciate more if I had some skin in the game. To this day I suspect they meant that literally.

My goal was to sell 200 boxes. As I confidently approached my first customer's front door, a beast as tall as the St. Louis Arch flattened me into a snowbank. "Don't worry, he's one giant teddy bear, a real softie," the owner chuckled. "And he likes you. I can just tell." I questioned the sincerity of that statement as the giant teddy bear punctured, shredded, and swallowed the plastic bread bags Mom put over my Moon Boots. All that for two boxes of Trefoils.

At the next house, I was pinned against the mailbox by a shark with overactive salivary glands. (The scar above my left eyebrow is still visible.) The lady gave me a wad of toilet paper to wipe the blood and ordered one stinking box of Do-Si-Dos.

When another savage charged in my direction, I hightailed it home and abandoned my dream of camp. You once wrote, "Guilt. The gift that keeps on giving." I would like to add frostbite, stitches, skin grafts, and the rabies shot vaccine series, which I had to undergo for the next fourteen days. I had skin in the game, all right.

Erma, I share this story with you because Girl Scouts don't hustle anymore. Kids in general aren't expected to pour their blood, sweat, and tears into fundraising because their parents do it for them.

What is most insulting is that they don't even ask in person. Instead, coworkers leave order forms casually laying around the break room. Or acquaintances make heartfelt pleas on social media with links to their PayPal and Venmo accounts. "Help support dreams and passions!" it might read, followed by a trail of patronizing smiley faces, hearts, kissy lips, and winky eyes.

In the past three months Hank has supported the passions of his boss's twins, Fennel and Sage. He subscribed to a weekly soup delivery service to fund a glamping trip and bought a 72-piece set of adult coloring books to hire a professional choreographer. If that wasn't enough, Hank felt pressured into sending a care package to his secretary's rescue potbelly pig at fat-acceptance camp.

If an industrious moppet with an order form, pen, and hopeful eyes rang my doorbell this minute, I'd run and get my checkbook. But I guarantee that will never happen. And even if it did, no one accepts checks anymore.

Yours truly,

Me

THE GREATEST GENERATION?

Dear Erma,

I'm afraid my flaring temper toward Gen Z may be the sole cause of global warming. My favorite quote of yours is, "Worry is like a rocking chair: it gives you something to do but never gets you anywhere." Although truer words were never spoken, I lose sleep obsessing that those responsible for making *Baby Shark* the #1 most-watched video of all time will eventually oversee nuclear codes, build secure bridges, and insert catheters into the urethras of those I love.

This afternoon I got stuck in traffic due to a catastrophic wreck—a protest. I couldn't tell what it was about because the signs were written exclusively in emojis, which has been declared the official language of the United States for those 25 and under. Prior to that, this demographic spoke entirely in acronyms such as IKR, ROFL, LOL, IDK, LMAO, and YOLO when their penchant for conjoining words such as shacket, jeggings, and Brangelina still proved too time consuming. (If they ever get jobs and have familial responsibilities, perhaps then they might understand the meaning of FMLA and finally learn to STFU.)

I had no choice but to park my car, sit back, and watch the show. The show could have passed for *Joseph and the Amazing*

Technicolor Dreamcoat based on the motley sleeve tattoos inspired by subway graffiti and neon hair dye the shades of *Sesame Street* puppets. You should have seen their piercings! Their earlobes resembled the mouth of the scary figure in *Scream* by Edvard Munch. JCPenney's drapery department doesn't have as many grommets.

My eyes were drawn to a gal fastening a scarf around a tree trunk. Her knitting tote read, "Addicted to fair-trade, responsibly sourced wool," with an image of heroin syringes to look like knitting needles. A hipster wearing a Mr. Rogers-ish outfit and a heavily pomaded man bun announced, "Birthing people Nature called," and skipped to the unisex loo.

Maybe it's just me, Erma, but if I had to go badly enough, I wouldn't pass on a perfectly good auto-flush toilet with rose-scented seat covers. In Nam, my dad took plenty of dumps in sandbags, then burned the waste in fifty-five-gallon drums while suffering trench foot and trying to avoid Agent Orange. But this virtue-signaler chose to take a stand by refusing to sit, a futile act of defiance that would only damage his own colon. I had a hunch that if he were desperate enough, his passion project would quickly be reprioritized from a #1 to, well, a #2.

Along the way he fist-bumped a gal wearing a tank top with TRIGGERED BY PATRIARCHY! embellished across the chest. "Daddy," she cooed into her rose gold Apple watch, "will ya DoorDash me a lychee milk boba tea?" Do not even get me started on these delivery service apps. Meals-on-Wheels used to be the only way to get food delivered to your home, but only if you had the misfortune of suffering from a chronic health malady. Sometimes, after the death of an immediate family member, a sympathetic neighbor might drop off a casserole, but then you had to go to the trouble of returning the dish. And now, boba tea. *And Daddy!* All I can do is SMH and think *WTH?*

At this point, a driver honked his horn, a micro-aggression the protesters deemed "toxic." It is interesting how that word has regained popularity in recent years. When I was their age, it used to be the motivating fear factor behind changing tampons at regular intervals, as the TSS insert warned. It once described deadly materials such as nuclear landfills, lead paint, asbestos, and the poison Mr. Yuk ingested. Now "toxic" is an insult given to those with the audacity to indulge in a differing opinion.

Soon, another driver nailed on the horn. And then another. And another. Then I, too, was among the feisty honkers overtaking the block party. I felt as if I was in the opening scene of *La La Land*. Road-raging felt so good!

One poor young activist, however, appeared to be on the verge of a nervous breakdown. She tightened the leash of her emotional-support ladybug holding a tiny placard that read: DON'T ASSUME MY GENDER. Then she grabbed her phone from her back pocket and speed-dialed a number with such hostility that the screen protector cried out, "Ouch!"

You would not even believe what happened next. Right there, amid all the chaos, she had an emergency therapy sesh via

Zoom. Although I didn't recall hearing any tornado sirens or announcements from the National Weather Service to hunker down in the northwest corner of a windowless room, she left to seek shelter in a "safe space." For her, that was the Infinity Flavors ice cream shop.

There used to be four choices: chocolate, vanilla, strawberry, and Neapolitan for indecisive people. Now there are bizarre flavors, such as dill pickle, balsamic vinegar, and wasabi. (For those preferring unflavored, there is White Claw.) So, imagine my surprise when she came out of the store empty-handed and demanded the shop shut down immediately. Why? Because they used plastic sample spoons!

This cancel culture stuff is out of control. The owner of my favorite pizzeria once served time for money laundering, but boycotting his pies would only be punishing myself for someone else's mistake. I'm not stupid. Besides, money laundering was how he kept his prices so low. Think, people, think!

Anyway, the next thing I knew, an Infinity Flavors employee stumbled out of the shop past the "heroes work here" poster and collapsed on the sidewalk. Even though he worked a two-hour shift in air-conditioning, the attending EMT diagnosed him with exhaustion. You would be led to believe he was a Great Depression-era potato farmer or Meghan Markle's public-image consultant. *Exhaustion!!!*

A flurry of activity caught my eye. An influencer and her camera crew came to livestream the event. Such fun! (I will give credit where credit is due, and I applaud her for proving my parents wrong about algebra being a necessary life skill.)

They pushed an unhoused individual out of the way who held a sign that read, SPARE ~~SOME LOOSE CHANGE~~ A TWENTY? then commenced filming. Groups posed for the cameras with their mouths wide open, unconcerned about blowflies laying eggs on their molars. I'm sure they were only trying to show off their perfect smiles whitened from charcoal toothpaste, but did they ever look like nincompoops! There is no reason for that unless they were getting tested for strep throat or eating a Chipotle burrito (when they haven't run out of food for the day).

What I cannot understand is why they add an extra syllable at the end of every sentence as if an exclamation mark. If the Twin Towers collapsed today, they would grumble, "OMG-ahhhh. When will T-Mobile and Verizon get their Wi-Fi back up-ahhhh?" They also add the word "hashtag" at the end of their sentence as a CliffsNotes version of what they just said. It's maddening. Overhearing them chitchat is the Sunday equivalent of hearing someone speak in tongues at a church service.

After the medical brouhahahahahahaha, the crowd dispersed, and traffic finally began to flow. The elderly man ahead of me, who never once honked his horn, inched forward to reveal his bumper sticker: THE GREATEST GENERATION. I wondered who could possibly argue with that, but I think we both know the answer.

Yours truly,

Me

P.S.: I'm sorry if *Baby Shark* is now stuck in your head. That song is toxic-ahhhh.

HELL ON A SHELF

Dear Erma,

Years before COVID-19, China released another insidious experiment into the world: Elf on the Shelf. Welcoming one into your home is more of a commitment than subscribing to Comcast.

Let me explain the concept. EOTS is Santa's mouthpiece, a Christmas version of the White House press secretary. It claims historical significance for being 1) the only thing in America with a body mass index in the normal range and 2) the first doll to officially use they/them/their pronouns. (Elliot Page has implored Metro-Goldwyn-Mayer's DEI committee to change *Ben-Hur* to *Ben-He/Him/His*.)

Throughout December, every night after children have fallen asleep, the EOTS flies round-trip to and from the North Pole. The purpose of their voyage isn't to accumulate frequent flyer miles but to suck up to their boss, Santa Claus. (In spite of checking zero luggage, Spirit Airlines tacks on hundreds of dollars in fees.) Tattling, of course, is typically frowned upon but children reluctantly accept such behavior in hopes of receiving an Xbox, PlayStation, or Nintendo Switch. (The only switch I ever got was across my backside from my Great Aunt Maude right after calling me a "cheeky whippersnapper.") If the young'uns weren't so gift-obsessed, they'd have learned that stuffed, cloth-covered snitches get stitches, lots and lots of stitches. But I digress.

Standard attire is a modest red leotard with a white dissent collar exactly how Ruth Bader Ginsberg (may she R.I.P.) dressed for Jazzercise. The smirk on their silicone face is exceedingly punchable. Except for Scott Peterson, no one has nailed the smug look so effortlessly.

Erma, when my parents sent me to college, their only rule was that I call home on Sundays after 6 p.m. when long-distance rates were cheap. But this felt toy has all sorts of conditions:

> 1) They are allowed to listen but not speak (much like Bianca Censori).
>
> 2) They are never to be touched or else risk losing their magic. (A virginity myth if I ever heard one.).
>
> 3) They must be repositioned into an array of amusing scenarios on a nightly basis. The more extravagant the shenanigan, the higher the expectation that tomorrow's stunt will be even more entertaining. (This creates an endless cycle of doom, similar to Kanye West's social media posts.) This is a toughie to keep up, Erma. I don't even have the time or patience to watch *The Crown.*

You once wrote, "There is nothing sadder in this world than to awake Christmas morning and not be a child." I respectfully object. There is nothing sadder in this world than to awake on a December morning at 2 a.m. from your husband's snoring and realize you forgot to move the EOTS, so you drag yourself out of bed to wash the dirty spaghetti tongs as quietly as possible then reposition the ~~little bastard~~ delightful holiday addition without establishing physical contact, which gives you flashbacks of playing *Operation* with your sister, who tried to startle you when retrieving the wishbone, and thanks to her you now suffer with chronic anxiety.

You may wonder why I take part in such nonsense if it's such a hassle. Well, much like March Madness brackets and Fantasy Football leagues, participation is mandatory per our HOA association board president. I hate her.

Sometimes, no matter how hard I've brainstormed, fresh ideas elude me. In such cases, I consult the maniacs who have made it their life mission to create outrageous vignettes using clothing and accessories worthy of Carrie Bradshaw. *The New Yorker* has reported that this creative outlet has become popular with retired *Dancing with the Stars* costume designers.

~~If~~ When nothing inspires me, our EOTS adopts a more practical mindset and performs ordinary household tasks. ~~If~~ When George calls EOTS "lame," I simply explain they are trying to be a helpful elf. Mommy has a lot to do, and Daddy is waiting in the man cave for the Ugly Christmas Sweater Party to begin at the oxidized-avocado-colored house.

How did things get so out of hand? My siblings and I used to leave Santa a cup of room-temperature powdered milk and a paper plate with burnt, broken, stale cookie bits. Now Christmas Eve entails climbing onto an icy rooftop to lay out platters of non-GMO carrots for the reindeer. Vixen and Dancer, in particular, need the calories due to their side-gig as sex workers in the off-season.

Christmas isn't the only holiday that has become "extra." The Easter Bunny leaves a trail of Jasmine black pearl tea balls disguised as faux poop before hiding a basket full of Stevia jellybeans. The St. Patrick's Day leprechaun conveniently forgets to flush his green pee down the toilet (which can happen to anyone after a night of Bailey's). The tooth fairy has even been known to dole out hundred-dollar bills. (Not in my house! George gets a buck; zippo if it has a filling.)

I have to admit, it's bittersweet knowing these traditions won't last forever. Part of me doesn't want my son to grow up. Another part looks forward to the day I can just settle down for a long winter's nap like Clement Clarke Moore intended. *That* would be a Christmas miracle!

Yours truly,

Me

THE FINAL LETTER

The Office of the United States of America

Postal Service Corporation

Dear Me,

As our last remaining customer, we are extending a professional courtesy to inform you that we are permanently ceasing operations. Many factors contributed to this difficult decision, as detailed below.

First, we are unable to overcome production challenges. Our SMART-sorting equipment is incapable of processing envelopes typed exclusively in emojis and acronyms. Additionally, it's confusing when the name of the addressee, street, and city are the same.

Secondly, our agency is experiencing unprecedented labor shortages. Many senior team members have taken leave to get plastic surgery, attend therapy appointments, and pack school lunches, which take an immense amount of time. As expected, our talent acquisitions department has indicated that no one from Generation Z has applied to our multiple employment postings. In the interim, we adopted a flock of rescue carrier pigeons, which were highly effective in performing many core duties. Unfortunately, they tend to get disoriented in neighborhoods consisting primarily of grey houses, which represent 96.04 percent of our territory.

Third, safety is of paramount concern and a matter we do not take lightly. Staff have reported numerous incidents of distracted drivers taking selfies, drinking coffee, removing shapewear, and coloring. Free-range children and designer dogs have also assaulted them. Our entire fleet has sustained extensive damage from titanium testicles and recorders smashing into their windshields. Regrettably, our crowdfunding efforts have not proven successful.

In summary, our business model is no longer sustainable. Gender-reveal party invitations, meal-delivery subscriptions, and course catalogs account for a small percentage of our annual revenue. The total and complete cessation of handwritten thank you notes and personal letters further depleted our cash reserve. Enclosed, you will find a bundle labeled:

RETURN TO SENDER. Undeliverable as addressed to:

Mrs. Erma Bombeck

Woodland Cemetery

118 Woodland Avenue

Section 201

Lot 395

Dayton, Ohio

45409

We have taken the liberty of finding the recipient's X handle and are providing it at no cost:

@thegrassisalwaysgreenernoverthepearlygates

It has been a pleasure to serve you, and we are grateful for your support. Remember to be happy and choose joy, because as Erma used to say, "Those who laugh, last!"

Sincerely Yours,
The United States Postal Service Corporation

ACKNOWLEDGMENTS

From the depth of my heart, I offer my appreciation to…

My dear, loving, humble, gorgeous husband, Steve, for providing me with uninterrupted writing time in my itsy bitsy office tucked inside our pantry. You are lovely in every way, and you will always feel new to me. I love you, babe.

My darling boys, Alex and Charlie, the absolute loves of my life. I couldn't be prouder of the young men you are becoming. The world is a better place with you in it. Remember, words (or the lack of them) matter. I love you more.

The Gs, the funniest, quirkiest, and most interesting clan ever to exist. Our personal family jokes fill my life with laughter. Your unconditional acceptance makes me feel whole. DO DO DO DO xoxo

My supportive, loyal friends across the globe who assured me this day would happen. Extra hugs to Kate, my soul sister and fellow crime junkie, for catering my book launch in epic style, with your wonderful husband, Steven.

The entire team at Flint Hills Publishing, for making every step of the process a delight. President, Thea Rademacher, thank you for believing in my work and making my dream a reality. Your professionalism and passion for the publishing industry are inspiring. Vice-President, Sandra Gore, you make multitasking and organizing look like a cinch. Editor, Anne Spry, I appreciate you embracing my sense of humor. Cover designer, Amy Albright, your talent is sublime. I am not sure I will ever come down from this cloud.

My encouraging first editor, John Briggs with Reedsy, your verbal Red Bull took my manuscript to the next level.

Mike Reiss, your generous cover blurb means the world to me. Thank you for not exploding on the Titan; you have many jokes yet to write, and I cannot wait to read them.

The Bombeck family. Thank you for taking the time to read my manuscript, providing such kind endorsements, and for sharing your mom with America. Thirty years after her death, her legacy remains vibrant as ever.

The Erma Bombeck Writers' Workshop family. The three magical words Tom Price said to Erma applies you as well. "You can write." Teri Rizvi, you are a credit to the organization and cheerleader to all. I will never forget when Anna Lefler called with the news that I had won the "A Hotel Room of One's Own" residency. That white, fluffy bathrobe has opened so many doors, and I will be forever grateful to everyone.

The legend, Alan Zweibel, who gave me the most valuable writing advice ever received: "First put up the Christmas tree. Then add the ornaments." What a gem!

Lucy Childs and the Aaron M. Priest Literary Agency, Inc. whose permission to use Erma's quotes added the perfect element of nostalgia to this book.

The Writer's Colony at Dairy Hollow in Eureka Springs, Arkansas, where my body, mind, and spirit were nurtured by delicious food, nature, and the company of fellow artists with similar goals.

Mrs. Brasch in heaven, the only high school teacher who gave me an A+ on every assignment and encouraged my gift. I hope you are proud.

Erma Bombeck in heaven, your light continues to shine on the world. How I wish we could have met.

My darling mama in heaven, who instilled in me an appreciation for the simple things in life—this book's theme. To have a mother who comprehended the intricacies of my sensitive heart and traced the minutia of my complex, dreamy soul is a gift every child deserves. Being your daughter was my greatest blessing. xoxo

ABOUT THE AUTHOR

Jillian Van Hefty is an award-winning humor writer and essayist whose work has appeared in *Chicken Soup for the Soul; Sisters! Bonded by Love and Laughter;* and many other publications. In 2022 she was grand prize winner of the "A Hotel Room of One's Own: The Erma Bombeck | Anna Lefler Humorist-in-Residence Program." She lives in the foothills of the Ozark Mountains in Northwest Arkansas with her husband, two teenage sons, and emotional-support Keurig.

www.jillianvanheftyauthor.com

www.ingramcontent.com/pod-product-compliance
Lightning Source LLC
Chambersburg PA
CBHW021127070726
47591CB00014B/1687

* 9 7 8 1 9 6 6 3 2 3 5 5 6 *